Are You Sure You Don't Like Reading Poetry?

John William Skepper

Dip Ed BA upper class (hon)

A.H. STOCKWELL
PUBLISHERS SINCE 1898

Published in 2024 by
John William Skepper
in association with
Arthur H. Stockwell
West Wing Studios
Unit 166, The Mall
Luton, Bedfordshire
ahstockwell.co.uk

To my late wife, Maureen – a gracious lady and an adoring wife to me for sixty-five years.

Contents

1: Are You Sure You Don't Like Reading Poetry?

Are You Sure You Don't Like Reading Poetry?

Poets are human beings too so, reader, bear this in mind.
Modern poets have a message and their poems are so designed
To communicate with other beings who deign to read this verse,
Overcoming the school-formed prejudice, which oft proves to be a curse.

Poets use poetry to communicate and it's always been the case
But Shakespeare, Milton and others brought teenagers little solace.
For passing English Lit exams, poetry oft creates disillusionment
As poems have a different concept when read for pure enjoyment.

Poets don't always convey their thoughts in a form simplistic
And, true to tell, poetry can be very individualistic.
Yet modern poets try exceptionally hard their feelings to relate
As one of their priorities is to communicate.

Poets are from all walks of life and age is no deterrent
That's why their poetic output is mainly so divergent,
Varying from the humorous to themes which are emotional
Through seriousness, via speculation, even to the notional.

Poetry usually has a message which one can understand
But before one can extol its virtues, one must join the growing band
Of armchair poetry readers, then perhaps one will comprehend
That poems are more than rhyming verse
and can be a consoling friend.

2: My Life in Reality or How I Imagine It

It's Never Too Late

Oh, how I regret those days of yore
In the prime of my happy schooldays
Not taking the chances so generously offered,
Being idle in so many ways.

A seat at the back, my position in class.
Helped me to turn a deaf ear
To the wisdom and knowledge destined for me.
I was young and could 'catch up' next year!

My homework completed in record time
I was free to accompany my mates
And we mis-spent our youth at the billiards hall
Where fun reigns… work procrastinates.

Of course, on the games field I thought I was king
Being gifted at most manly sports.
Receiving respect from my peer group for this
Whereas 'swots' get sarcastic retorts.

I hated exams and detested the work
To be revised at the end of each year.
It fuelled my dislike of science and maths,
English Lit killed my love of Shakespeare.

After examinations, the school report came
Well sought-after by all the form's 'goodies'
As for me, I might be school centre forward
But I was certainly right back in studies.

How often in this life it is a truism
That one and only appreciates the real meaning of 'chance'
Long after the opportunity has gone
For it rarely occurs more than once.

My 'sporting activities' practised at school
Are now no longer pursued.
I've adopted a different slant to my life
With a desire for learning renewed.

My craving for qualifications is clear
And I need to make up for lost time
So I'll take up my options with the O.U.
For I'm hardly out of my prime.

If it takes me six years to complete the course
And a BA degree would be fine
I shall then consider my knowledge complete
And I'll still be only 89!

My First Girl Friend

I went to Scarborough for my hols,
and I walked along the sand.
The cries of a distressed damsel I heard so I
thought I would lend her a hand.

She was out of her depth, just off the coast,
and the waves were ten feet or more.
I dived in dressed in my brand-new shorts
and brought her safely to the shore.

She was so grateful and readily agreed to
meet me at the 'Fisherman's Rest',
Where I embarrassed her with my first remarks
"I hardly recognised you dressed!"

Her features were harsh and she weighed twenty
stone and the way she spoke was quite coarse.
She descended from the Vikings
and so had a face like a Norse.

I kissed her once upon the cheek
and gave her a couple of hugs.
She was due to start her new job the next
week as a model for Toby Jugs.

I called for her just after 7am.
It was a case of 'Toujour L'amour'.
Dad opened the door in his pyjamas! What
a strange place to have a door!

I went to the dentist with big Gert. She was
one of life's losers, no doubt.
She was told that her teeth were just perfect
but her gums had to come out.

She was wearing a red dress and matching hat
next day, on the prom, where I met her.
She opened her mouth to shout an 'Hello' and
a young boy tried to post a letter.

To say she was big was an understatement and
I understand just what she meant
When she said she did not shop locally. She
brought her clothing from 'Rent-a-Tent'.

I soon got tired of big Gert
and gave her a farewell kiss
But she did not bat an eyelid
and countered by telling me this:

"When attributes were doled out at birth
I was the last in the line.
And as they gave out human brains I thought
they said 'trains' and missed mine."

"Noses were next given out
but 'roses' I thought was the call!
So I said make mine a blooming red one and
my nose now lights up half the hall.

"Ears were the next on the list
and I thought beers were the award
So I asked that I should have two very large ones
– I supply wax to Madame Tussauds!"

"Finally, they allocated chins,
which caused me no end of trouble.
I thought I heard someone say 'gins'
and greedily ordered a double."

"So, with features so strange and so lewd I
cannot hope to stay with one guy.
I need a new mate, my tale to relate and I
wish you good luck and goodbye."

Innate Scrabble-Ity

My wife and I play Scrabble and it really is a tease
For our approaches to the game are dissimilar as chalk to cheese.
Whereas Maureen plays defensively and strikes me on the break
My modus operandi seeks a maximum score to make.

Whereas Maureen takes her time and patience dictates her game.
I gamble on picking the right tiles, '7 out' being my aim
My method to be truthful, rarely obtains for me the score
Enabling to me to claim a win. It's happened many times before.

Last night, after losing yet again, I retired to bed so tired
And I dreamt I was in a Scrabble game and my enthusiasm was fired.
The difference in scores was forty plus with mine the smallest total.
To say this was 'par for the course' would merely be anecdotal.

In my last play, using tiles, I made the small word 'new'
And I groaned almost audibly at replacement tiles 'Z and Q'.
But wait! Perhaps these were not too bad as I had 'U' on my rack
And with the game still in its infancy, here was a chance for fighting back.

I checked my seven tiles and the vowels were 'U', 'A' and 'E'.
Leaving four consonants to make up my word, namely 'L' 'Z' 'Q' and 'J'.
My thoughts were now in overdrive, composing a word in my dream.
And I sensed there just might be one to restore my self-esteem.

But was there a place on the board to fit my chosen word?
I nonchalantly raised my eyes… and then I, literally, stared
For not only would my word link with the 'S' of 'files'.
But, there were doubles as bonuses for both my 'Q 'and 'Z' tiles.

On my rack I arranged the letters my selected word to test out
And as the letters fitted so neatly I wanted loudly to shout.
But instead, I calmly added 'QUETZAL' to the Scrabble board
Gloating to myself of the hundred and sixteen I had scored.

'Quetzals,' with the two doubles, gained for me a sixty-six score
And for using all my seven tiles I scored fifty points more
Which gave me a handsome lead. It is fortunate I'd heard
Of the Quetzal, a very under-rated Central American bird.

Isn't This Where I Came In?

When I was born I didn't have any hair upon my head.
My eyes did not focus properly, or so my mother said,
I was washed and changed regularly and given liquid feeds
Relying solely on others for all my basic needs.

At the age of five I left home. Oh, life can be so cruel!
And for the next fourteen years I spent most days at school.
From being an only child and my parents' pride and joy
I had to share with others. A fact bound to annoy.

At eleven years my 'Scholarship' admitted me to Grammar School
Where I worked hard, mostly, but sometimes 'played the fool'.
Suffice to say that this school separated 'sheep from lambs'
And when I reached my leaving day I'd passed all my exams.

The obligatory National Service provided discipline to my life
And in my early twenties I chose myself a wife.
A life-long career in teaching became my chosen vacation.
The Open University appealed to my imagination.

Studying for my credits was just a hobby for me,
Resulting in the award of an Upper Class Honours degree.
I served on local councils as an elected member
And served the public handsomely, as far as I remember.

When I finally I retired I thought could do worse
Than try my hand at writing a little rhyming verse.
Success in this came quickly, bringing me adulation,
For I soon found my poetry was fit for publication.

Now I am older I do not have any hair upon my head.
My eyes don't focus properly and I'm confined to bed.
I am washed and changed regularly, my memory misleads,
Relying solely on others for all my basic needs.

Ale and Hearty

As I lie under the table in the bar of the 'Three Tuns' Filey
I realise that I cannot continue to live 'the life of Riley'.
For one thing my purse is bare and friends treat me like a leper
But a more important reason is that my real name is Skepper.

Today's been very bad and there's no hope for tomorrow.
I only came into the pub so I could drown my sorrow.
I've mixed my drinks and you know you cannot win.
When you mix real ale with whisky, rum and gin.

I'm usually a practical beer-drinking, sober chap
But I changed quickly when I suffered a mishap
And now I'm legless and daren't try to stand upright
For I feel quite sickly and I must look a rare sight.

The reason for my sorrow is my wife's wayward trend,
As this morning she left me and went with my best friend.
For weeks they have been friendly and last night I saw her kiss him.
So my best friend has taken her and, oh how I do miss him.

We were inseparable at the pub and always drank real ale.
He always had a merry quip and he could tell a tale
To keep you laughing. Although of late he'd made excuses
Saying that he could spend his time for better uses!

I've been a fool and doubly so.
I've lost my wife and reached a new low
By drinking spirits with my beer.
And instead of more I feel less cheer.

The moral of my tale is clear.
"If wifeless, stick to wholesome beer,
"Don't behave as though you're beyond the pale."
But face the future with real ale.

A Window on My Life

When I look out of my window
What is that I want to see?
Is it a street, field, woodland scene,
Or is it, perhaps, the sea?

In my 'teen' years the view was poor
As I lived in the midst of a street
And my outlook was a built-upon area.
From my casement window seat.

Not that the view really mattered.
For when I stayed in at night
I was busy doing homework
And sat there for advantage of light.

Other times I'd be out of the house
Spending unearned 'pocket pence'.
And, for sure, the view from home
Was of little consequence.

When I 'got wed' my status changed,
But, we both, our jobs did keep
So the bungalow was less a home.
More a place we used for sleep.

We had little time to sit and gaze
At the view of the country scene
And the bay windows in the bungalow
Were just more glass to clean.

Time did not let us appreciate
The restful, rural calm
And our working and social commitments
Took preference over idyllic charm.

But with ever increasing age
And retirement on its way
We looked for a coastal French window
With an open view over the bay.

At long last we have an abode
And the time, to a certain degree,
To sit in our coastal bungalow home
With a window overlooking the sea.

I Am What I Eat

Two years ago the nurse told me my cholesterol level was high
And every year, from coronary heart disease alone, around 170,000 die.
Excess cholesterol in the bloodstream can block blood vessels to the heart
So she advised me the action to take and a low lipid diet start.

I was given several leaflets which I examined for a while
And I learnt my high cholesterol was due to genes and my lifestyle.
I could not change my genetic make-up, I had to accept that,
But, with a careful diet, I could reduce my intake of fat.

My diet sheet indicated food I should and should not eat.
It was a complete list from fruit and veg to drinks and joints of meat.
I was not too surprised to learn that my diet had to change
And, henceforth, I would have to eat foods from quite a different range.

Gone were white rice, crisps and crackers and I was to avoid white bread.
I would change to wholegrain cereals, wholemeal loaves and brown rice instead.
Choosing a main course without excess fat meant chicken, veal, turkey or rabbit
But no duck, goose or crackling from pork, I'd have to 'kick the habit.'

To control my life's excesses it only takes strong will
But there's an additional incentive if such excesses make me ill.
When searching supermarket shelves for foods to help me 'crack it'
It's well worthwhile to take my time and read what's on the packet.

Should I make excuses why my diet I can't keep? I'm cheating
Only myself. For most stores stock supplies designed for 'healthy eating'.
Eating between meals is a habit I must try to break
For I only end up eating biscuits, chocolates or iced cake!

So when I'm really hungry and fancy a tasty dish
I avoid all dairy products, settling for fruit, lean meat or fish.
I've refused to buy confectionery, excess alcohol is out
And I'm beginning to feel much healthier, of that there is no doubt.

By having my cholesterol level measured regularly by the nurse
I can ascertain whether dieting has served its main purpose
And should the level have been reduced, for that is my hopeful guess
I'll have conquered my erstwhile craving for unhealthy food excess.

Careering Through Life

During my school holidays when I was in my teens
I always took on part-time work to augment my means.
The local Inland Revenue always offered me a job
And so I learnt quite early how to earn an honest bob.

Without my casual vocational occupation
My expenses over income would have made the wrong equation.
At Christmas when I needed more to make my life complete
I became a temporary postman rather than just 'walk the street'.

Next came my National Service and I fought like any pro
For my right to stay in civvy street but I still had to go!
I then went into industry with evening classes for further knowledge
And was absolutely delighted when accepted for Training College.

A teacher I became and spent hours in preparation
If my wife had not been a teacher too it could have led to separation!
Promotion came in stages as I progressed to Department Head
Where I taught children History, so my job description said.

Through Deputy Head to Headteacher I progressed in course of time
And when retirement came around I devoted my life to rhyme.
Publishers were very kind, accepting my rhyming verse
And, as a budding poet, I could spend my time much worse.

My employment experiences I use to very proud good effect
In poems which, hopefully, will avoid the dreaded reject
Slip. So far, with my success, I am modestly well pleased
When one's hold on one skill loosens then another can be seized.

Poetry has worked for me yet others may get different urges
As long as one searches for it, one's chosen skill soon emerges
And, as a retirement hobby, it is better than regular employment
For it provides both satisfaction and a great deal of enjoyment.

My Life Initially

I was born in Gainsborough, Lincs in 1930 AD
A citizen of the UK in the part they call GB
My schooldays ended with my SC followed by my HSC
I enjoyed my weekend camps undertaken with the ATC
I'd been brought up as a Christian being baptised in the C of E
My cricketing days saw me playing for the Wanderers CC
I served my NS with the RAPC
Where I reached the rank of corporal bringing in more LSD
To train as a teacher I went to the Leeds City TC
My education being completed with an OUBA degree
And with the darker nights because of wartime BDST*
I successfully canvassed as a Councillor for Gainsborough UDC
I gained promotion in education, eventually becoming an HT
So I joined the HAHT union affiliated to the TUC
I usually shopped at the CWS and the GPO
Although my best friend has not told me I know I suffer from BO
I've had my IQ checked and Mensa has accepted me.
Should this lead to a promotion it means more PAYE
In my dotage I will settle for watching BBC TV
Before I 'pop my clogs' which will be my RIP.

BDST British Summer Time

My Artistic Creations

I PAINT pictures which tell stories and PORTRAITS of my life.
They depict bygone life of people, myself and, perhaps, my wife.
Paper is my canvas and for a 'brush' I use what's handy
And sometimes, for inspiration, I top my coffee up with brandy.

My ART describes the LANDSCAPE as clear as any STILL LIFE scene
And a careful choice of title shows my aim is genuine.
For the PICTURE conjured up by an artist in full flow
Can cause emotions which ignite a spark in another's libido.

By using rhyme with reason I can COMPOSE a MASTERPIECE
Which is MUSIC to my ears when I find it scans with ease.
In truth, BALLETIC MIME in my art form plays no part
But it could, perhaps, provide a theme for OPERATIC ART.

PLAYS abound which use my art in a theatrical setting
And once displayed upon a SCREEN it prevents us forgetting
The words which AUTHORS carefully choose to tell an involved story
Or re-enact events which become part of one's history.

By SCULPTING words and phrases to make the exact 'bon mot'
I create a place in LITERATURE to which like-minded wordsmiths go
To seek the relaxation to which only RHYMING VERSE gives rise
For it's in POETIC WRITING that my artistic talent lies.

Memory Is a Faithful Friend

Memory is a faithful friend as life's zenith one does reach
It is uniquely personal and a precious gift bestowed on each
Individual. Memory can shut out bad events highlighting just the good,
And the most dear reminiscences are oft of one's childhood.

The days of innocent youth, before responsibilities take their toll,
Are remembered as the halcyon days, and one is always loyal
To the memory of loving parents. One's house was then a home
And colourful past happenings replace what were merely monochrome.

Coal fires were a feature and the hearth shone with black lead
And, I remember with affection, the brass knobs on the bed.
In the kitchen was a copper 'Dolly Tub' and stone sink too:
For ablutions we had an old tin bath and a freezing outside 'loo'.

The gas light lit the parlour but on candles upstairs we relied
And, as we did not possess a car, it was on cycles we had to ride.
In front of a flaming coal fire we sat till our bare legs burnt red
Before we braved the chill air in the bedroom and the cold sheets on the bed.

We looked forward to Saturday evening when Father came back from the shop
For he brought back digestives and chocolate as well as a bottle of 'pop'.
On Sunday, for lunch, we had roast beef which we ate without saying a word
For, in those days, all good little children had to be 'seen but not heard'.

Pocket money was only a few pence as it was all that our parents could spare
But we spent it with careless abandon, blasé as any millionaire.
We used the front room for special occasions notably when company came,
And they sat drinking tea on our best settee, one-upmanship the name of the game.

I remember my formative years with a mixture of pride and regret.
Proud there are so many good things my memory does not forget.
However, my innermost thoughts cannot help me but dwell on the crises
And it's then I begin to realise how my parents made great sacrifices.

Teenagers were young and too busy to dwell on the kindness of others
And it's only much later in life that we appreciate our debt to our mothers.
They provided the love and care that enabled us all to thrive,
How sad that we never had time to thank them when they were alive!

It Is My Resolve

I make a resolution every new month of the year
And try to make it simple and not too hard to bear
For just as one lone swallow, a summer does not make
How can one resolution a year-long mission take?

In January I vow that all sunburn I'll avoid
And when the Christmas cake's all eaten I'll not be annoyed.
I vow, in February, to give up drink on the thirtieth day
And even if the sun shines I'll not make any hay!

I'll not celebrate the Ides of March, which signalled Caesar's fall
And I'll certainly not go sailing if the sky foretells a squall.
I won't let April showers make me melancholy
For, if I go out for a stroll, I'll take my golfing brolly.

I'll resolve to dress most warmly until the month of May is out
For I've often heard it said that one should not 'cast a clout'!
While June is 'bursting out all over' I will stay at home.
And examine all the job adverts with a 'fine toothed comb'.

Independence Day, in USA, is the fourth day of July
So I'll join the celebrations and try a piece of 'apple pie'.
The holiday month of August is when others tend to roam
But, as I have no money, I promise to stay at home.

September sees the days grow shorter and the nights are long
But I'll resolve to persevere with my September Song.
October starts the winter and puts me in a spin
'Cause it's the month for revolutions when the proletariat win.

The national Lottery's anniversary, November heralds in
So I think I'll have a flutter in the hope that I can win.
December brings us Christmas with all its joy and cheer
When I think of resolutions for another brand new year!

My Favourite Things – an Inventory

Memories of a happy childhood which seem so long ago,
Real winters when the roads were blocked with white and crispy snow.

The lingering light of the day before the horizon claims the sun,
The gleam in children's eyes when you know they're having fun.

The yeasty smell of home-baked bread, cooling on the hearth,
And the feeling of vitality when one emerges from a bath

The sight of bulbs in springtime as they burst forth from the soil,
The satisfaction of a job well done, after honest toil.

The fragrant scent of blossom from the apple and the may,
The sheep minding their little lambs as they gambol and they play.

The aroma of the flower beds after a shower of rain,
The balmy nights of summer when long days are here again.

The peaceful feeling created by the satisfaction of one's life,
The realisation that one is lucky to have a caring, loving wife.

The wholesome taste of a hearty meal with which to start the day,
A loving kiss and a friendly smile to dispatch you on your way.

My poodle waiting for me with a real-tail wagging greeting,
The warmth of double-glazing, combined with central heating.

A meaningful and genuine, complimentary word of praise,
The reference to one's past life recalling successful days.

The freedom to control one's life which retirement alone can bring,
The delight to be awakened as the wild birds start to sing.

The warmth and cosiness of home which two, or more, have shared,
The accumulated keepsakes which outshine the spoken word.

The sound of placid waves lapping o'er the sandy shore,
With the shrieking of the seagulls as a constant overture.

An upholstered, comfy chair and a book I have not read,
And, when I am exhausted, the sanctuary of my bed.

All of these, and many more, to me some happiness brings,
So they all must be included in a list of favourite things.

There Is No Fool Like an Old Fool

I like to think that I am a wit and
my humour sophisticated and acute.
However, in my heart of hearts I know
that my jokes are not all that astute
For they are more akin to the schoolboy's wisecracks
which most teenagers enjoy
And at which we guffawed behind
clenched hands, the teacher not to annoy.

Wherever I go and whatever I do,
I see the funny side of life
Which keeps me sane in retirement
but bores my long-suffering wife.
I crack corny jokes, deliver plausible puns
and try to steal the scene
At social gatherings. My jokes may not be very clever
but at least they're always clean.

When invited to a social gathering,
my childish streak assumes control
And to make others laugh and enjoy themselves,
purports to be my goal.
Although my motives may not be altruistic
when examined to the Nth degree
For I obtain great satisfaction myself
so I'm nurtured egoistically.

The truth of the matter is plain to reveal
as I've never matured as a wit
And I bore the pants off my neighbours and friends
as I really don't know when to quit.
What's more I do something which is inexcusable,
the typical trait of a bore,
I laugh at my jokes and show real bonhomie,
as if I'd not heard them before.

Kind adults may sometimes humour me
but children regard me with disdain.
That's how I know my humour is childish
for they feel I transgress their domain.
They do not know whether to laugh or cry
at my woefully feeble patter
So they simply manage a sickly smile,
thinking I'm as mad as a 'hatter'.

Why don't I accept that boredom reigns
when I perform my party piece?
Why do I persist in carrying on
when the glances suggest I should cease?
Why do I take the advantage
when the audience is a captive one?
Why do I feel elated
when the thanks I receive is none?

The truth is very simple
because I still have the childish belief
That the cares of one's life can be banished,
fun being the cause of relief.
And I hope the straight faces
conceal the geniality that I awaken
For I will continue my infantile jokes
until I am forsaken.

In at the Deep End

Being at school in the forties when World War was at its height
We had to make do with austere provision as the Authority budget was tight.

I suppose we were lucky to obtain what we did and to have this chance to learn
For had we lived in a war-torn city there would have been more concern.

I attended the local Grammar school where we were conscientiously taught
All the main academic subjects and we were not deprived of sport.

We had extensive playing fields, adjacent to the school,
But for all swimming tuition we relied on the town swimming pool.

The 'baths' as we all called them, were a mile and a half away
And, as there was no transport, 'there and back' took half a day.

The swimming baths were ancient and the cubicles austere
So we always stood on duck-boards for verrucae were the fear.

A cavernous echo reverberated around the spacious hall
But it's the pungent smell of chlorine which mainly I recall.

As we entered the shimmering water it always seemed so cold.
But to duck one's head was warming, if you dare to be so bold.

Even when walking in the shallow it felt just like slow motion
And non-swimmers would feel as insecure as if it was the Atlantic Ocean.

Learning to swim from scratch seemed an obstacle so immense
For it was not just learning a skill, it was gaining confidence

To let oneself go. When one eventually learnt the technique
It provided access to all water sports which most sporting types seek.

But why was it that the cubicles were so dark and dour?
And when you returned to dress it was your clothes on the wet floor?

Why did our fingers feel so numb, that it nearly made us cry,
So that our shirt buttons we couldn't fasten or our shoelaces tie?

Although I regard my schooldays as in the main, convivial
My memories of the swimming baths must appear to you quite trivial

And that is a shame for, for in truth, I was certainly taught a skill
Which allowed me to become a swimmer. A skill which is with me still.

Are We Always Blameless?

Who do you blame when things go wrong?
Do you rationally seek the cause
Or do you randomly allocate blame?
Is the fault ever yours?

You did not leave the light on
Or fail to lock the door.
Before accusing others
Do you make absolutely sure?

Do sound reasons prompt your judgement
And is your conscience always clear?
Is it other's fault you break things?
Is 'being responsible' what you fear?

Your dog being playful
When it receives its ball
But if it treads the plants down
Doesn't your throw count at all?

When proved wrong in an argument
Do you meekly eat humble pie
Or do you make pathetic excuses
As your blood pressure surges too high?

When someone asks you a question
The answer to which you should know
Do you admit your lack of knowledge
Or prevaricate to conceal IQ low?

In a crowded room if you chance to break wind
Do you own up and apologise
Or join with the masses and upturn your nose
Showing disgust and awesome surprise?

The Government of whatever persuasion,
Is it always to blame in your eyes?
You want spending on health and education
Yet you complain at every tax rise!

So the next time you make a mistake
Don't attempt to pass on the blame
But own up with a good grace
And hope others will do the same.

To Live to Be Old Is a Bonus

My imagination knows no bounds when I meditate
And fantasy takes over for a while.
It is then my spirit soars above body frailty
And I achieve my goals with finesse and some style.

As we gradually approach the period of old age,
An unpalatable time in which to live,
It is surely made more bearable to endure
When we consider old age's one alternative.

I will never win the hundred yards on a racing track
And to hurry is often difficult for me,
But I've been known suddenly to make a spurt
If I fear I'll arrive late for my tea!

I do not venture out of doors in windy and cold weather
Because the temperature is low when near the sea,
But I can still manage to enjoy life to the full
By watching all my favourites on TV.

If years are a criterion I must admit I'm old
Though my active brain's undiminished from my youth.
My senses and emotions are alive for all to see
But my joints and muscular strength 'long in the tooth'.

I can hold a conversation on topics quite diverse
If there's anyone out there with time to listen.
Although my voice is softer and slower to respond
And my frame is fragile, odd and somewhat wizen.

My eyes are not as bright as they were as a youth
But my inner vision helps me to survive,
For experience is a safeguard as one warily wends one's way
And my memories make me glad to be alive.

My hearing aid serves me well when my batteries aren't flat
Though I can lip-read when the speaker's near.
I also have the benefit of feigning temporary deafness
If there's something said I do not wish to hear.

Although I have less energy than in 'days of yore'
When I think of my actions in my prime,
I wasted much energy on dubious pastimes
Many of which were just a waste of time.

A young boy to his grandparents said
"To me you're more precious than gold,
"But one question puzzles me more than the rest
Why have you both to grow old?"

Growing old is not something to fear or regret
As it comes to us after a lifetime
Of memorable experiences, often too many to mention,
Be they horrendous or exhilarating, sad or sublime.

Down Our Street

There was laughter and joy and a carefree air
And our childhood life was so complete.
We had none of the trials which later life brings
Down our street.

We played sporting games and we played as a team
And when tired, the causeway was our seat
Because whatever the season there was always a warmth
Down our street.

We offended the neighbours on countless occasions
And at times were less than discreet
For we failed miserably 'to be seen and not heard'
Down our street.

We played seasonal games which we thought were harmless
Whipping-top, marbles, snobs, 'trick or treat'.
But we always remembered to be most polite
Down our street.

We were straight, true and honest, that's as I recall,
And we played fair, never attempting to cheat.
There was no referee when we played outdoor games
Down our street.

We respected the law, being scared of the police,
Avoiding them as they pounded their beat,
Although we were not guilty of doing any wrong
Down our street.

Artistic Desire

I wish I had a real artistic skill
So I could paint a picture with deft strokes.
I would approach my canvas with a will
And with my oils and palette depict folks.
My brush strokes would reveal their inner fears
Whilst capturing a child's mischievous smile
Or showing cause for a fond mother's tears
And the loneliness of the aged and senile.
Perhaps only in a truly visual form
Will comprehension mean something to me
For tattered clothes don't keep a body warm
And appreciating grief needs empathy.
Artists depict what, in real life, is true.
Painting encapsulates their point of view.

The Lament of the 'Would-Be Poet'

I wish that I a poem could write
With scansion, rhyme and reason.
I've tried my best for three score years
And in the Autumn Season
Of my life I'll make one final effort.
To see my work in print,
Even though it may be read by few,
Would make me feel omnipotent
And lead me on to further skills.
If reading poems is restful for the mind
How much sedation comes to him
Or her whose sentences are so designed
To formulate a tale in rhyme?
I worked and played and worked some more
But with censoring here, amnesia there,
What my life's been is 'just a bore!'
My thoughts abound and yet I know
My failure's clear. I've downed my chips
And it's not worth submitting this
To add to my 'rejection slips'!
But it's been written… so send it in.
My will to win's sincere and plain
For all to see. If not accepted
So be it! I'll just sit down and try again.

3: Humorous and Nonsensical

What's Their Line?

There's the chap who sticks the labels on the apples.
It's a pippin of a job, you must agree.
But the labels are not sticky, for no adhesive is used,
So he licks them, but there is no extra fee.

There's a man who puts the letters into all the seaside rock
And for that he needs, at least, an Honours degree.
If his geography was weak or he could not even spell
We'd end up with rock from Skunthrop-by-the-sea!

There's a firm that makes spirit levels for the whole joinery trade
And one woman is more important than the rest.
She has to make the bubbles which do such important work
And, in truth, she always does her level best.

There's a schoolboy who at school always wore a dunce's cap,
Teachers regarded him as 'thick' and made no bones.
Now he's a self-made millionaire with a few thousand to spare
And he can't produce enough of traffic cones.

Where would be without the unique polo mint?
Off-shore fisherman still suck them in their shoals.
All power to the elbows of the mint manufacturers
And let's hope they never ever run out of holes.

Butchering is an honest job and butchers tried to help
During the Depression years when times were hard and bleak.
Families could afford. at best, only a poor sheep's head
So the butcher left the eyes in to see the family through the week.

The public toilet cleansing operative has a most important job
In improving client relations, in my view.
But the assistant to the gaffer deserves our warmest praise
As he will conveniently be known as 'Number Two!'

Just Like That…!

When he got up each morning, in the bathroom he would grin
For he need not stick his neck out, not with his protruding chin.
As he pondered in the mirror whether to give the 'job' to BUPA
He realised that without it, he would not be Tommy Cooper.

He was concerned about his career which he regarded as a mess
And discussed it with his wife, over breakfast, 'Fez to Fez'.
He felt it was not funny as his magic all went wrong
And he dreamt of parts in films, as a sequel to King Kong.

But after he had eaten his despondency he forgot
And begun to practise magic but he crazily fluffed the lot.
So, with a nervous chuckle and a stare that would amaze,
He created his own gimmicks as well as his catch phrase.

On stage he tried to make out he was as crazy as a bat
But his clever repartee made him famous 'just like that'!
Tommy was never vulgar and his jokes were crude but clean.
No one could beat his clumsiness with his 'many hats' routine.

Once you'd seen a Tommy Cooper show you remained a loyal fan
For he was known in 'star' circles as the comedians' comedian.
To make you rock with laughter he only had to come on stage
And laughing at his own jokes was real wit from a sage.

Tommy had a massive frame and stood o'er six feet tall.
Towering over lesser mortals, he gained respect from one and all.
He was a friend to all he met yet often had a bout
Of comedians' depression, emanating from self-doubt.

So, if I had the chance of being someone for a day
My choice would be a star with whom I was 'au fait'.
I would enjoy my role and for me it would be super
To soak up the applause as the zany Tommy Cooper.

Opening Your Mouth... and Putting Your Foot in It!

We make a lot of 'faux pas' in our life upon this earth
But, why is it, when we make them that they create so much mirth
Amongst the crowd assembled? Sympathy's not their intent
As we hastily try to rectify to save embarrassment.

Yet, often, our attempts the situation to reverse
Only prolong the outcome, making matters even worse.
When I espied a long-lost friend when travelling on a plane
I shouted across 'Hi Jack' but I won't do that again.

Should you slip on some spilt beer but do yourself no harm
Yet a burly seven feet navvy similarly slips but breaks his arm
Don't laugh at his misfortune and, if you feel you have to chat,
Whatever you have to say to him, never say "OK I did that!"

When in the road outside your house, a gaping hole appears
And you call a community meeting to allay everyone's fears,
Remember it is serious and introduce no wit
As you surely will if you comment 'We're looking into it!'

If working in maternity refrain from cricket talk
Because an expectant father has sharp hearing, like a hawk.
As he paces up and down his thoughts can easily run amuck
If you mention to a friend "Two out... and one's a duck!"

When the train came to a grinding halt from explanations I did refrain
For I'd mistaken the communication cord for the toilet chain!
In truth, folks will stare and eye you with a certain condemnation
If you enter this 'small room' while the train is in the station.

If a faux pas you wish to avoid whatever is your age
Allow your thoughts to clarify before you 'take the stage'.
Remember, what you say is what your audience hear
So don't give your voice full throttle while your brain's in second gear!

999 Family Farce

The ambulance men walked into mayhem
When they answered a midnight call.
It should have been a routine 999
But they never know what may befall.

An elderly lady had made the call
After falling and breaking a bone
And, not wishing to disturb the household,
Summoned help by means of the phone.

The ambulance men duly arrived
And came into the hall to her aid.
Then seeing she needed some hospital care
Preparations for a stretcher were made.

As the first-aiders carried her out
Her son woke up from his sleep,
Collapsed unconscious from the shock
And crashed down the stairs in a heap.

The noise of his fall down the stairs
Disturbed his slumbering wife
Who came from her room to the landing
And was confronted with this scene of strife.

The mother-in-law was being carried away
And her husband, lying prone, in the hall.
This was too much for her to bear.
She fainted and crashed into the wall.

The family dog was alerted by this
And thinking that they had invaders
Decided to show he was a house-dog
And attacked one of the first-aiders.

This 'family farce' has not been made up.
I would not compose such affliction.
But I quote the events as they happened that night
Proving fact is much stranger than fiction.

A Girl Named Fred

A girl was born to the family 'Bear'
She was born bald but she had some hair.
The tresses which ran down her back were red.
Tis a pity that they were not on her head!

A beautiful girl she was christened Fred
And the warts on her face turned many a head
Her clothes were made by a couturier
So everyone used to call her 'threadbare'.

Fred was a tall girl of three feet eight,
Kept appointments on time, always being late.
With her friend she ran races indoors all alone
And wore out the carpets, of which she had none.

When the snow was raining it was odds on
She'd run barefoot with just her clogs on.
She was a tuneful singer but had no voice
And was forced to work hard, of her own choice.

There was no gas supply to the village of Hayter
So she put all her spare cash in the meter
During the night she enjoyed the sun's ray,
The moon coming out in the middle of the day!

Skills of reading and writing she had none
So she went to Oxford and became a Don
She travelled by train, which was a real pity,
As she never dared venture outside of the city.

Fred married a man with no head for heights,
A steeplejack, who stood up for his rights
Of wooden legs he had but two
And Fred loved him dearly when the divorce came through.

She bought a dog which she called 'Kitty Kat'
But never fed it so it grew quite fat.
She next bought a cat and called it 'Rover'
And used it on the bed as a nightdress cover.

She had 'green fingers' and liked to grow
Flowers and plants for the horticultural show
There was none where she lived but it really was a shame though
When the odd-jobman knocked her 'box' off the window.

As a keen athletic type she favoured field events
And when she picked the javelin up, excitement was intense.
As well as opening the event she very nearly shut it
And she would have put the shot but forgot where she had put it!

She became claustrophobic for a number of years
And shut herself in a box to overcome her fears
Fred bought all her goods through mail order, as a norm,
But her address never appeared on any order form!

Finally she retired inland on the coast.
She had no children and of them she would boast.
Fred died of old age at the age of twenty- four
And the rest of her life was really a bore!

Wellie No' Come Back Again?

One day last month my wellingtons I left outside the door.
I didn't think twice about it I'd done it several times before.
I always take my boots off when entering my home
And my grievance I will relate in the form of this short poem.

I know that today's youth are very much maligned
But on opening my outside door I was surprised to find
That the two boots I had placed there had been reduced to one
And so I grew suspicious as to where that boot had gone.

It was a Tuesday evening when the weekly Youth Club meets
And perhaps someone had 'borrowed' it to take part in great feats
Such as hopping around the Village Hall or perhaps just wellie throwing
Or maybe some more devious ploy, there certainly was no knowing.

And that is why you may have found me 'hopping mad' that week
For walking in one wellie surely made me quite a freak.
But all that now has ended and I have some boots to wear
For last weekend I went out and bought myself a brand new pair.

I now have three good wellies and to the thief I say:
"Why not admit your guilt and another visit pay
If you can prove that you are broke but must have both feet shod
I'll sell you my spare wellie cheap and homeward you can plod."

You see I know that owning three can be a dubious joy
Yet thinking about it even more, I have another ploy.
I'll leave all three outside my door and this can be my plan
For if they all should disappear, I'll blame the 'Isle of Man.'

It's All in the Mind

My life is unadventurous, I'm a sedentary chap,
But my imagination knows no bounds when I sit and have a nap.
After a hearty meal and in front of a glowing fire
I become a cross between Walter Mitty and Waterhouse's Billy Liar.

One night I entered a crowded lift, because stairs are such a bore.
The lift set off quite quickly but did not stop at the top floor.
When I saw stars I realised that this was just my stage
And my knowledge of sci-fi films allowed me to land the cage.

On a charter flight from Heathrow there was a slight mishap
When, without any warning, the tailwing began to flap.
I slid down the fuselage while others gazed. struck dumb,
And I managed a repair job, thanks to my chewing gum.

I went to catch my commuter train at twenty-five to nine
Only to find it halted by Autumn leaves on the line.
I had to think of something in this hour of the rush
So I volunteered to bumper-ride with a very wide yard brush.

The thrill of parachuting has been surpassed by the free-fall.
The feeling is 'out of this world 'and you have no fears at all.
Halfway down I realised that I had no parachute
But my golfing umbrella proved an adequate substitute.

Marooned on a desert island with a motley shipwrecked crew
Who were totally exhausted and, as survivors, had no clue
Yet I was able to save them, which may have come as a surprise.
I gave them all a copy of Golding's 'Lord of the Flies'.

I rode in the Grand National in a field of thirty horses.
As every jockey knows Aintree's the exemplar of courses
At Becher's Brook I was last, as it was a furious pace,
But after twenty-nine had fallen I trotted home to win the race.

So all you would-be adventurers, whatever your occupation,
Don't despair if you don't get the chance, you've got your imagination.

Hello, Hello, Hello!

I was speeding along on the motorway
Passing everything in sight
When a police car came up behind me
With its siren and flashing light.

If I was breaking the speed limit
It certainly was unwitting
And it did not disturb my passenger wife
Who passed the time by knitting.

I reduced my speed accordingly
And moved over to the slow lane
The police then drew alongside me,
Their objective was quite plain.

On a motorway I knew not to stop
But one PC yelled "Pull over!"
I glimpsed at my wife who was knitting still,
And replied "No, a coat for Rover".

Rover, my dog, was on the back seat
And clearly had had enough.
He decided to vent his thoughts on the police
Which sounded to be "Rough rough!"

Eventually, a slip road came into view
So I took it and came to a halt.
Two policemen approached from their Panda car.
They thought clearly that I was at fault.

"Do you know what speed you were doing, sir?"
Said one PC who winked at his mate.
"I have an important appointment," I said,
"It's important that I am not late."

"Oh come, come sir!" the PC exclaimed
"You'll have to do better than that!"
"Now tell me why you were clocking a ton.
Perhaps you've come out of hell? You're a bat!"

My wife then decided to say her piece.
To tell the truth she was intent.
"We were hurrying, officer, cause of poor brakes.
We don't want an accident!"

The PCs pondered, nodding their heads,
"That seems likely ma'am. We won't nag.
But before we allow you to go on your way,
PC Brown, go and fetch me the bag."

The PC was back within a trice,
"Please breathe into this bag that I've got."
"Is this a breath test?" I calmly enquired.
"Don't be daft! Our chips are too hot."

When told to go, we soon sped from the scene
With no sadness, rage or remorse
But with thoughts of compassion shown on that day
And a pride in the British Police Force.

Dedicated to Participating Patisseries

In the two Great Wars the English bravely fought against the Huns
And all the Service personnel were fathers, brothers, sons.
The one thing which kept them sane, as they defended with their guns
Was the thought that once back in civvy
street they'd be eating sticky buns.

From early times some women have shown
strength which others shuns,
The best example being the powerful Amazons.
To achieve their goal of muscle tone they went on lengthy runs
To the nearest bakers who supplied their sticky buns.

Woman may devote their lives to God and become nuns.
They live in lonely convent cells or, perhaps, in close-knit communes.
The meals are plain but wholesome and mostly a nun shuns
All types of fatty pastries, apart from sticky buns.

If you have a reservation you must live with Red Injuns.
The excitement is 'in tents'. Please excuse the corny puns.
The faces on the totem poles resemble harridans
Who are suffering from sharp stomach
pains through eating sticky buns.

The House of Parliament consists of the Lords and the Commons
Where MPs' recorded speeches in the Hansard is weighed in tons.
Often their forthright comments, even the Speaker shuns
But, later, they meet together for a drink and sticky buns.

4: Sport and Pastimes

Pastimes of Past Times

To keep our children happy and provide them with real pleasure
It's important that they are taught how to spend their leisure.
The network and computer games may suggest sophistication
But a disadvantage does accrue, involving isolation.

Modern activities tend to be devoid of integration
Between two or more. There is no chance for organisation
By an individual over members of his peer group. Keen
Though one may be in competition with the monitor screen.

What happened to those games outside, played by two or more,
Like marbles, conkers or hopscotch, with
the 'pitch' chalked on the floor.
Remember table soccer which could be played by one and all
With old pennies used for players and a 'tanner' for the ball?

For those who enjoyed games with participating 'masses'
There was 'rusty bum' for lads and 'kiss catching' pleased the lasses.
And even when individual games tended to be in the ascendance
They were usually played with onlookers closely in attendance.

I played with my 'yo-yo' and 'snobs' and, hereabouts, they do say
That 'whips and tops' were produced to celebrate on Shrove Tuesday.
And should you live near water, like calm seas, rivers or lakes
Bouncing 'skimming stones' across water
was known as 'ducks and drakes.'

Two games I still remember are now not played at all
I refer to 'egg if you move' and a game known as 'long ball'.
In both, a tennis ball was thrown and a hit was a kill.
Three 'kills' in the former game and you went 'through the mill'.

All the games mentioned above could be played out-of -doors
And I am sure we were much healthier and needed fewer cures
For minor ailments. If your 'den' you never leave
You will miss out on companionship, fresh air and 'joie de vivre'.

The Playground Beckons

The playground beckons
The conglomerate herd
Where lively children play
And differences are blurred.

The whistle beckons
Adult normality
Received by youth with silence
And grave formality.

The classroom beckons
Where learning is the rule
Within the edifice
That everyone calls school.

The lunchtime beckons
When a beefburger and 'shake'.
Take precedence over work
And stems the stomach ache.

Then home time beckons
Where love and care exist.
But what of those who live
Where none is manifest?

Where a home lacks care
Children count the seconds
Longing for the morrow
When… the playground beckons.

Seasonal Pastimes

Is it my imagination or do games to seasons correspond
When in my youth I played out in the street or perhaps beyond?
Certainly some of our activities needed suitable weather
For winter is not the appropriate time to hear willow hitting leather.

The arrival of the ice and snow saw toboggans appear
From their summer storage and downhill we slid without any fear.
Bare hands made snowballs from snowflakes
But later we would suffer from the hot aches.

For the lassies, if not the lads, spring saw the advent of skipping
And everyone was welcome if one was quick enough to nip in
But the experts had to be light of foot and a consistent stepper
To maintain the frenzied pace of 'salt, mustard, vinegar, pepper'.

On Shrove Tuesday we'd hardly time to eat a pancake ere
We'd be outside with whip and top, also known as 'window breaker.'
Another game played out of doors on hill tops or in the valleys
Was a game played with marbles known colloquially as 'glass alleys'.

Football was also a favourite sport with goalposts chalked on the wall
For boys would kick most anything and, sometimes a football.
But for boys and girls, Hide and Seek is the game which still endures
And they enjoy the nightly search until time to go indoors.

If You Can't Beat Them... Why Bother!

He enjoys all sports and cannot wait for seasonal ones coming round.
His approach is quiet confidence, with both feet on the ground.
Whether it is the cricket square, bowling green or tennis court
He knows that he will be acclaimed as a conventional 'good sport'.

When facing demon bowlers he fearlessly stands his ground
And fielding in the slips his hands are regarded as quite sound.
In soccer he takes the penalties and he's never missed one yet
And he's equally at home as custodian of the net.

When bowling on an outdoor green he invariably hits the jack
And on the snooker table he's adept at potting black.
His tennis serve, on grass and clay, is a real revelation
And with a hockey stick he is admired throughout the nation.

The athletics track he burns up in distance runs and sprints.
The shot he only put once but hasn't seen it since.
When jumping he achieves success, whether it be long or high
And the way he clears the pole vault takes him nearer to the sky.

As a jockey he's outstanding and he does it all for kicks
As he races the tracks of England on the first flat over the sticks
And on his polo pony there is not a hint of shyness
As he peruses his opponents, looking for his Royal Highness.

At Formula One, eventually, he hopes to make a kill
When he shares the track with Schumacher,
Villeneuve and Damon Hill
And on his motorcycle he has yet to meet his match
As he whizzes around the hairpins to victory at Brands Hatch.

Who is this unique sportsman? Hasn't he got a name,
As he tours the various stadia in his incessant search for fame?
He is any one of countless men, lounging on a couch at ease,
Using television imagery to fulfil wild fantasies.

5: Nature

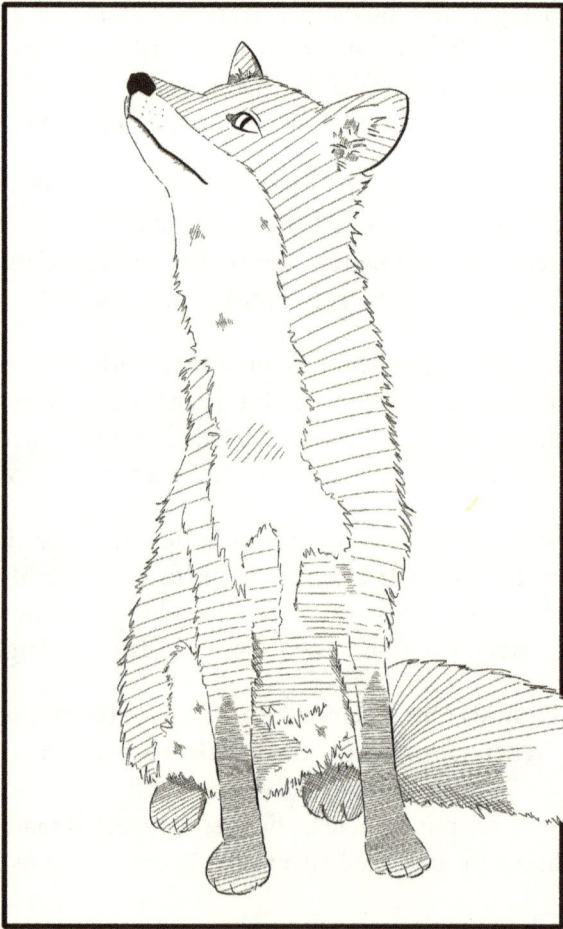

Woodnotes Wild

'Wild animals' suggest animals with a savage temperament
Conjuring up, in the mind, quite the wrong sentiment.
Such animals, for the most part, are comparatively mild
And a better definition is 'Animals which live in the wild'.

Even the human being can fly into a rage
But no one suggest for that they should be banished to a cage.
Treating all creatures humanely should be the basic key
So that animals in the wild can naturally roam free.

Out on the open range where the mournful buffalo roam
It may be quite extensive but to them it is their home.
To imprison these beasts permanently would be quite absurd
For then they would, most certainly, hear 'a discouraging word'.

The lion is a noble beast and, notably, full of pride
But in a circus or zoo cage there is nowhere to hide.
When asked to perform unnatural tricks to satisfy adult and child
Is it surprising that it becomes more 'ferocious and wild'?

Russian pandas, with black eyes, in foreign zoos look so cowed
Is this, perhaps, because they object to mating before a large crowd?
Their refusal to do so may be why they look so glum
But the keepers should thank their good fortune there's no 'panda-monium'.

As for eating grandmothers most wolves are not all that partial!
But how often are human opinions formed, based on circumstances farcical?
Remember the well-recorded spider which inspired Robert Bruce, by chance.
Now all arachnids are credited with extra powers of perseverance.

So here's strength to the elbows of the W.C.S.
Which is making giant strides to relieve animals from stress.
Please rally and give your full support all you generous 'guys and gals'
To make life much more comfortable for the 'not so dumb animals'.

The Miracle of Nature

The natural world is governed by the vagaries of the seasons
And each one is important for a multitude of reasons.

The spring and the summer epitomise the blossoming of life
While in autumn and in winter we witness hibernation rife.

Spring may be the finest season which we enjoy on this earth
For, in all of nature's life forms, we begin to see new birth.

Spring flowers bloom and, all around, expectancy's in the air
And leaves and blossom cover trees which winter had laid bare.

The sun in summer has the heat to nurture nature's stock.
It also brings refreshing rain to quench its thirsty flock.

Summer sees the growth of the new-births from the spring.
The time when all the crops do grow. No wonder wild birds sing!

Autumn heralds the approach of potential winter sights,
Bringing shorter days and the longer, colder nights;

Autumnal colours from deep red to various shades of brown;
With strong winds 'getting up' and the spent leaves falling down.

Winter has frost as a feature and sometimes a blanket of snow.
Hibernation is nature's answer, in the lands where cold north winds blow.

Food for wildlife is at a premium with everything laid bare
And it's a real fight for survival to try to get one's share.

Spring starts nature's annual cycle at the Vernal Equinox
When the dormant life of winter, nature instinctively unlocks.

The growth of animals, plants and trees are beautiful to behold
Until the Autumnal Equinox begins to turn green leaves to gold.

The quality of human life is enhanced by nature's miracle
Of rebirth and re-awakening, because nature is empirical.

The lambs at play, the birds that sing, bring pleasure at every age.
The blossom and flower gardens are backdrops for the world's stage.

So, whatever nature proffers always treat with veneration
Then the miracle can be enjoyed by every generation.

The Twentieth-Century Urban Fox

Stealthily, cunningly, ever aware of the slightest of passing dangers,
The urban fox, that ace marauder, has to contend with the human 'strangers'.

They do not understand the fox is merely hunting to survive.
In the hearts of men it strikes a fear of wild attack, should it stay alive.

Yet almost the opposite is true because the fox, by nature shy,
Has hardly ever attacked man, who seem determined it must die.
A fox is but a minor cog in nature's instinctive food chain
And, though it's been known to kill for food, it dines on wildlife in the main.

Indeed, so timid is the fox that it ignores the cat at play
And should the latter start to fight, the urban fox oft runs away.
It hunts for mice, worms, birds and voles and rarely ever roams in packs
But tends to feed vixen and cubs on throw aways from human snacks.
It's genuine fear of human threat sees it venture out when the coast is clear

And, as this usually means the night, not many see the fox appear.
A family may live 'neath your shed and play on your lawn in the dark
But, if the 'food' is plentiful you'll seldom hear the fox's bark.
A handsome creature is the urban fox, recognisable by its bushy tail,
And, relatively, harmless to mankind. Let's hope that man's death wish will fail.

To exterminate the urban fox is killing for killing's sake
But perhaps, with a more reasoned view a 'domesticated' friend we'll make.
However, should we deign to try, man's attitude to it must change.
Then fox and man can live in peace and both may find it rather strange!

Jack *Snipe*

I've recently moved house to a rural neighbourhood
And my next-door neighbour, Jack, has been by me, misunderstood.
He keeps the strangest hours and he has so many friends.
He seems to take whole weeks off work and he's away for most weekends.

So what can be his *hobby* of which he keeps me in the dark?
Is it drinking *kestrel* lager or *skylarking* in the park?
Or perhaps he flies a *red kite*, though that is hard to *swallow*.
Or does his little *stint* at the *Dotterel* inn, with a sandwich *tern* to follow.

He goes *swanning* off most weekends but I dare not ask him why.
You see, I've interfered before a case of once *bittern*, twice shy.
He may be visiting *his turtle dove*, his little boy or little *gull*
Or as a *gannet*, dining out to make sure that he is full.

He often looks a little *ruff* in his scarf, gloves, hat and cloak.
But his liking for warm clothing suggests an open-air type of bloke.
And here, perhaps the mystery of his irregular movement lies
For he could be one of the many fans of Newcastle FC's *magpies*.

To visualise a more sombre cause really gets my pulse a-throbbing
For I hate to think he might be involved in burglary or *rob'in*
No, perish the thought, he could not possibly be a *crook*
For, if he crimes had committed, surely, he'd be brought to book.

I once heard him mention '*Mallard*' so a trainspotter he may be
Although, he also speaks of '*Goldeneye*', suggesting a James Bond devotee.
He fools about with all his mates and when they run amok
He is not averse to saying "you sound like a ruddy *duck!*"

Could he possibly be moonlighting to please the manager of his bank?
But what job needs a *yellowhammer* combined with a *redshank*?
If you still wish to know his *hobby* this poem in rhyme provides the picture.
Look at the words italicised. My neighbour has to be a 'Twitcher'.

Bempton Cliffs Reserve

On our regular excursions to Bempton
we are filled with excitement and glee
And the sights and sounds that surround us
are certainly more than just sea.

It's a bird sanctuary that we visit,
which the RSPB does maintain,
And once you've found Flamborough Headland
you surely will go there again.

Herring gulls are there in their thousands
with their grey backs and wings tipped with black.
And their red-spotted, bright,yellow bills
which allow them to snatch any snack.

There are maritime gulls, known as kittiwakes
which spend most of their time out at sea.
They have small heads and benign expressions,
flying lightly but so buoyantly.

You'll see gannets aplenty at Bempton.
In flight they're shaped like a cigar
And diving for fish, from a great height,
is a fine sight for all to savour.

The guillemot loves swimming and diving offshore,
a gregarious bird found in flocks.
It stands bolt upright when it reaches the land
and it breeds on the ledges of rocks.

The razorbills, blacker than guillemots,
have a deeper shaped bill, with white line.
In flight an elongated silhouette is seen
and for nesting, rock crevices are fine.

A small but most comical seabird has, perhaps,
the most real crowd appeal.
I refer to the popular puffin
with its parrot-like yellow and red bill.

The puffins build nests in burrows
but, off-duty, loaf around the cliff top.
And their short, rapidly-whirring wing movements
give the impression that soon they could drop.

The fulmar's a heavily built seabird
at cliff-breeding colonies, gregarious.
It possesses a tube-nose and thick bull neck
and at harassing trawlers, it's notorious.

If this little poem has done no more
than to set the Bempton Cliffs scene,
Think how much more you'll appreciate it
when to see the seabirds you have been.

The Sights and Sounds of Bempton

Beady and cold eyed, riding windswept waves,
Fulmers, for seventy years, have nested on Bempton's coast.
It is a rugged coastline, dotted with bituminous-black caves,
Eroded by tidal action, of which the relentless sea can boast.

From mid-May to July's end sea-birds nest on the cliff-face.
Bright red and yellow parrot-like beaks denote the jaunty puffins
While razor bills and guillemots, back from the sea, return to base.
Standing erect like small dark brown and white penguins.

Shadowed cliffs drop sheer into heaving and swelling seas.
Myriads of white breasts perch without evident foothold.
Through field glasses bird-watchers see the huddled gulls with ease.
Then, showered from the ledges, thousands fly with cry and scold.

Raucous cries of gulls ring out, darting and wheeling in all weathers
Gannets and kittiwakes abound but we view, with some dismay,
Waste oil discharged on waters which coats gulls' flight-bearing feathers
But the puffins lay in burrows wisely keeping from harm's way.

Bempton's flinty, chalk-white cliffs are a sight singular and rare
And as bird sanctuaries go, is well conceived.
The RSPB administer it, with pride and loving care.
Why not pay a visit? You'll be well received.

The A... B... Sea of Life

For a fascinating day out and a visit to the coast
Why not come to Scarborough Sea-Life where you will witness most
Of the marvellous world of marine life and be
Intoxicated by the realism of life within the sea.

Sea-Life is intriguing with its stunning mature displays,
Both informative and exciting in so many ways.
The wildlife under water is a sight to take your breath away
And you will be so intrigued that you'll need to stay for half-a-day.

Technology is to the fore to stage this marine spectacular
But you don't need to be an expert to understand the vernacular.
As special presentations are programmed regularly
To inform you of the life which exists beneath the sea.

There is a multi-level viewing which ensure you see so much
And at Sealab and the touch pools you are even encouraged to touch
Spidery crabs and live starfish. Habitats become a plus
When they house the likes of seahorses and even octopus.

But new in '97 we can see Jurassic Seas
When you become a time-traveller and are transported at your ease
To a period in history when sea life first began
And the development from single cells is introduced to man.

As you pass through the cavernous walks with fish above your head
You imagine that you're travelling along the ocean bed.
It's relaxing and instructive and the memory you will keep
As you stroll through Sea-Life Centre with its mysteries from the deep.

It's a journey well worth taking, but give yourself good time,
For to miss out some of the displays would surely be a crime.
There are thirty plus to savour, each with unique appeal,
And I'll bet your heart will cry out when you see a rescued seal.

Magnus – The Mastermind

He may look quite ungainly as he waddles on dry land
But he swims with slick dexterity when there's food at hand.
Magnus is the guardian of the seal pups and no fool
As he basks his portly frame on the bank of the seal pool.

You'd think he'd be oblivious when the public come to view.
But he keeps a wary eye open, as all good guardians do.
The seal pups tend to show off, in the way of domestic pets,
As they recuperate from lung worm or the damage caused by nets.

The object of seal rescue is reinstatement, in the main,
As they hope that all these charges will return to their domain.
Magnus who is twenty-seven, has seen it all before
He appears to weigh five hundredweight and probably much more.

The visitors may consider that he thinks he's in a zoo
But he regards himself as viewer and the public his to view.
Because seals don't have taste buds they swallow herring whole
But their other senses are enhanced to keep them in control.

They need to be alert to survive in the wild ocean.
Their whiskers sense vibration of predators in motion
And their ears are extra sensitive to every passing danger
While their eyes can see through murky waters vetting every stranger.

Magnus is too old to be returned to the sea
You can tell that he's aware of this, yet is content to be
A feature of the sea-life pool where he has let them tame him
And, as he is fed regularly, you cannot really blame him.

6: Religious

God Is in His Element

When God created the earth and encouraged all forms of life
He chose the Garden of Eden to introduce man to wife.
Flotation into the universe had to be prevented
So, to keep our feet firmly on the ground, gravity was invented.

But of the existing elements, earth is only a quarter
And one should not forget the other three – fire, air and water.
Fire is needed for warmth, cooking, smelting and also drying
So God attended to basic needs by this element supplying.

He knew that humans and animals would have to survive adverse weather
And excitement was intense the first time two sticks were rubbed together.
God also provided the oxygen within the air we breathe
And gave us the means to extract it, another basic need.

For life depends on oxygen being present wherever we go
And God replenishes what we use to retain the status quo.
The greatest threat to mankind is a polluted atmosphere
But God is omnipresent so, of that, we should not fear.

Water, the basis of all liquid, completes the elements' quartet
And a shortage of pure H2O portends a real health threat.
The seas and oceans may be fine for those who guard our nation
But salt water cannot be drunk without desalination.

It is not coincidental that all basic needs exist
And I'm sure that when God made our earth he had a complete list
Of all the necessities for life on earth. Nothing was left to chance
Which could make living tolerable and the quality of life enhance.

The proof is here for all to see on God's designer earth
So what awaits for all his flock as we await rebirth?
The resurrection of our souls is the Lord's labour of love
And we shall reside in perfect peace in God's heaven above.

The Gifts of God... Too Numerous To Mention

It's the smile on mother's face when her new-born babe is whole
On the fragility of nature when you see a filly's foal.
The pride of doting parents as offspring attain degrees
And the loving care devoted to those with incurable disease.

It's the regularity of the sunrise, bringing warmth and light,
The belief in a supreme deity which lets us sleep at night.
The cycle of the seasons which accounts for Spring's new birth
And the satisfaction of believing that God controls the earth.

It's the composition of the elements which allows us to survive.
The feeling of contentment and the joy of being alive.
The knowledge that mankind has learnt to aid simplified living
And the feeling of wellbeing we achieve by selfless giving.

It's the thoughts that guide our actions when our conscience lends a hand
And the wisdom, bestowed by the Lord, which helps us understand
That all life has a purpose accumulating an annuity
So one can ensure after-life will be lived in perpetuity.

It's the senses which enable us to become so discerning
And the brain cells, when developed, responsible for learning.
The muscles, which keep us active, as our fitness we sustain
And the nerve endings which, rapidly, communicate with our brain.

It's the thought that we are on this earth to carry out good deeds
And the ability to recognise and to respond to other's needs.
The strength to appreciate the power of all things spiritual
And, within the divine kingdom, to agree that God's empirical.

God's gifts are all around us but too numerous to index.
Some are, by nature, simple and others are more complex.
But the significance of all gifts which God is willing to confer
Is that they're bestowed for all humanity, each entitled to a share.

God Lets Us Reap More Than We Sow

The passing years have taken their toll
and I ache in every limb.
My joints have stiffened somewhat
and my eyes are growing dim.
The days when my garden was beautiful
have now come to an end
For I cannot afford a gardener
and my garden I cannot tend.

I remember the roses in bloom,
a magnificent view met my eyes,
And the buddleia shone like a beacon,
a haven for all butterflies
The aroma of blossom was sweet
and the smell of the heather sheer joy
And the pond brought a haven of peace
for shubunkins, goldfish and koi.

Now the rose bushes have overgrown
and buds given way to bare thorn.
A coarse entangled grass has replaced
what was once an immaculate lawn.
The scent of the garden has gone
and the flowers have all gone to seed.
The fish in the pond are no more,
having succumbed to the dread blanketweed.

As God is a lover of gardens
mine must make him groan in despair
For he will remember it from days gone by
and to see it looking so bare
He must surely pity the owner
and sympathise with his plight
But I wish that he could lend a hand
to set my garden right.

He cannot, of course,
as that a miracle would be
And he does not gain his converts
by blatant bribery.
He prefers religion to flourish
because believers hear the call.
Then he'll be there to receive them in Heaven,
be they great or small.

So my garden God will not, actually,
till with a holy hoe
Yet in winter he will ensure it is covered
with a blanket of snow
Which shows me that at least,
he is doing his level best
To make people think that my garden
is as good as all the rest.

So do not blame God for one's failings
while living on this earth
For God is all-seeing
but does not judge your worth
On what you might possess.
It's the belief in your inner soul
Which makes Heaven your resting place
and allows you to achieve your goal.

Spiritual Apprehension

Lord, give me the faith that has alluded me so far,
The belief shown by the shepherds who were guided by a star,
The ability to know that there exists a God omnipotent,
For only when I possess real faith can I hope to be content.

Lord, as I make my way through life with a selfish greed,
Make me aware of others who have got far greater need
And let my erstwhile craving for materialistic wealth
Be replaced, for all times, with a spiritualistic health.

Lord, give me the strength and fortitude to believe that life is more
Than merely living on this earth our allotted span, before
We are taken to God's Heaven, where we dwell in perpetuity,
And our Christian acts alone are sufficient as gratuity.

Lord, turn my thoughts to greater things than seeking to have more
Of life's material possessions when I should be looking for
The real pleasure, beyond a price, to sooth my troubled mind
For the belief that there is a God outweighs all wealth in kind.

Lord, point me to the righteous path of truth and real salvation
And I will try to follow it without any deviation.
For on the 'straight and narrow' I will focus my true role
And my mind will be at peace as soon as I achieve my goal.

Lord, teach us to be tolerant and somewhat less defiant
And, as to worldly goods alone, let me be less reliant.
Fill me with spiritual belief which transcends selfish desires
And lead me to eternity to which my soul aspires.

Lord, I empathise with the lost sheep 'ere it returned to the fold
As I often feel that, spiritually, I'm left out in the cold.
So help me, please, to overcome my desire for things graven
And prepare myself for eternal life with you in highest Heaven.

Church Is Not Just for Solace When Disaster Strikes

What has happened to religion? Where is the Christian ethic?
Are churches becoming little more than an expensive relic
Of past glories? Their upkeep is a concern shared by all of the nation,
But donations for essential repairs relying
on a dwindling congregation.

Is it the pace of life which causes one to shun the Church?
Or is it our self-sufficiency borne of scientific research
Into the origins of life? Perhaps, when life is quite serene
One has less need on God to lean.

It is in times of stress or trouble one seeks a consecrated place
Where one can outpour one's hidden thoughts and hope to gain solace
Knowing that God, through the Church, will lend a friendly ear
As well as give us comfort and us to recovery steer.

Why then does not the Church attract the younger generations?
Is it lack of influence, save for special occasions?
After baptism, most people like their marriage to be blessed
And the next significant visit is when they are laid to rest.

In days of yore when Godparents their duties did not shirk
And parents had time for their children, with mother not at work
When schools allied with churches and taught the Christian creed
It was the religion had a meaning when adults gave a clear lead.

If shops and sport compete on Sundays with attendance at a church
I'm afraid presiding vicars will be left in the lurch
Facing only ageing Christians in their congregation
With an absence of any members from the younger generation.

What then can be done to reverse the situation?
The answer is not easy and it needs real inspiration.
It has to start with childhood, based on parental persuasion,
And followed up in schools with apt religious education.

Add to this church ministers with extrovert personalities
So that we don't rely on disasters with numerous fatalities.

Noah... The Ark Angel

When the fear of floods descended
upon God's mighty earth
The nation's manhood had the chance
to illustrate their true worth.
One man stood up to be counted,
working from dawn to dark.
His name was Noah
and his brainchild turned out to be an 'Ark'.

If the floods came he knew animals
would be taken unawares
So, for the purpose of reproduction,
he assembled them in pairs.
When the Ark was finished
Noah hadn't time to mop his brow
As he started boarding his charges
to maintain the status quo.

The animals were nonchalant,
with the Ark a haven of rest,
And exhibited their well-known traits
with more than usual zest.
Pigs were wallowing in discomfort,
missing the cosiness of their sty,
Camels cautiously contemplating
that elusive needle's eye.

The peacock was preening its plumage
while the elephants tried hard to forget.
An aardvark expounded its theory
that it hadn't killed anyone yet.
The zebras invented a crossing,
the serpents sounded as if they'd been knighted.
The glow worms insisted on a low profile,
lest they should, by Noah, be de-lighted.

Though the skunks were getting quite high,
the giraffes wished they were not so tall
And the gibbons were watching, with interest,
the Roman Empire's rise and fall.
While the donkeys made asses of themselves,
the mice simply gnawed on the planks.
St Bernards were chosen to represent dogs
and the only cats there were Manx.

The kangaroos had their paws in their pockets,
an expedient to keep themselves warm.
While the owls nodded their heads in approval,
hyenas laughed, as was the norm.
The hippos missed meals while watching their weight,
the turkeys chose to miss Christmas Dinner.
The cow set its target at getting the bull
but had to make do with an inner.
The ostrich had nowhere to bury its head,
the frogmarching was entertaining,
The buffaloes listened for 'discouraging words'
while the chameleons' colours kept changing.

But those animals forgot their differences
when they were made cosy and warm
And, with their support, Noah was able to embark
and eventually rode out the storm.

God's Kingdom

Spacious is the word to describe Our Lord's kingdom
For he has to keep a place for every Harriet, Dick and Tom.

Happiness is the atmosphere generated in God's Heaven
Where reality shines through and there is nothing which is graven.

Agelessness is soothing as time itself stands still
And everyone exudes rude health for no one there is ill.

Neighbourly bonhomie abounds and the spirit is set free
Where enemies do not exist and friendship is the key.

Grand with all its multivarious meanings is
The word which epitomises Heaven's utter bliss.

Regal describes the Celestial abode fit for the Heavenly King
And those who believe in the Lord will hear the angels sing.

Immortality with one's God is our destiny from our birth
And it's everyone's entitlement after a stint on this earth.

Leisurely life awaits us all in our Heaven in the sky
And we choose the pace to suit ourselves as we watch the clouds drift by.

All things to all people is God's heaven, our new home.
That is why a name is hidden in the contents of this poem.

Just take the initial letters of alternate lines so far
And you'll see I think God's Kingdom is the Christians' Shangri-La.

It May Take Time but It Is Worth It

Another second has passed my Lord
Since I, on bended knee,
Decided to confess my sins
And put my trust in thee.

Another minute has passed my Lord
Since I steeled myself to pray
To thee, my God, in Heaven
For like a sheep I'm prone to stray.

Another hour has passed my Lord
And I feel a sense of pride
That I have banished bigoted doubts
And with you I will abide.

Another day has passed my Lord
And I've begun to understand
That through all tribulations
You provide a guiding hand.

Another month has passed my Lord
And my once black hair is grey
Yet I feel like a two-year-old
Since I've begun to pray.

Another year has passed my Lord
When I've striven to attain my goal
And though my physical strength is weak
You've revived my spiritual soul.

Another decade has passed my Lord
And my life has a new zest
I've opened my mind to your good grace
And now realise I'm Heavenly blessed.

Small Can Be Beautiful

When searching for buildings consecrated to God,
Lincolnshire has many to savour
And although Lincoln Cathedral is architecturally unique
there is another church I favour.
Tiny Pilham Church is a little gem.
So small it can easily be missed
But as the Lord's house and a Haven of Prayer,
it proves a good catalyst.

The dedication of Pilham Church to All The Saints
is not purely by chance, I'm sure,
For, virtually, it is Gainsborough All Saints'
Parish Church in miniature.
There are some differences internally
but, perhaps, size is the reason for one lapse.
In the east end, instead of a chancel,
it boasts a semi-circular apse.

Its pinnacle tower and Venetian window,
however, are just the same
As the Gainsborough Church and thereby
it derives its fame.
It was probably built in the mid-eighteenth century
according to local history
But who actually paid for this replica to be built
appears to be a mystery.

The monument to the Reverend Dunkin
and his son, Theodore,
Conceals quite a few handed-down tales
but they tend to be mostly a bore.
Whereas William was rector for forty years,
his son was somewhat wayward
And, as chaplain with the East India Company,
he soon sought sanctuary abroad.

The interior of Pilham Church is white-washed
and normally quite neat
But the total length of this very small church
is scarcely twenty-four feet.
The original plain windows have been replaced,
as was the Victorian fashion,
By stained glass depicting the Crucifixion
and the instruments of the Passion.

Pilham Church is only tiny
and there are not too many seats
And it is no longer the central place
where a social gathering meets.
It's sad today that like most churches,
it relies on a religious 'hard core'
To support it financially
and keep the proverbial 'wolf from the door'.

Star Gift

I
AM
THE
STAR
WHICH
ADORNS
THE TOP
OF EVERY
XMAS TREE.
THE SYMBOL
OF THE STAR
WHICH MARKED
THE COMING OF
A DIVINE DEITY.
OF
ALL
GOD'S
GIFTS
BESTOWED ON THEE
THE GREATEST
BY FAR IS
ETERNITY.

7: Family Relationships

I Love You

I admire you for your courage in confronting life's nuances
And I worship your commitment to engage ambition's chances,
I admire your selfless nature when together we are thrown.
And I love the very thought of you when I am all alone.

Admiration stems from an understanding of your strengths
And true love negates weaknesses as the heart takes great lengths
To understate the foibles of ones 'amour' lest the wise head
The heart, should rule. Some things are best 'unsaid'.

Beauty is more than skin deep, emanating from the inner soul.
So worship and adoration of you becomes an appropriate goal.
But my lover must be educated in order to differentiate between
The complex and more trivia, the garish and the serene.

You fulfil all my latest desires with your qualities, oh so rare!
Your confident lifestyle enhances your appealing energy and flair.
To prove my intentions are honourable and my emotions are ever true
I'll encapsulate all my feelings and say simply: "I love you."

A Valentine Greeting

Love is a special word which is difficult to define.
It can be voiced in words or conveyed by the merest sign,

Such as a genuine smile or a long, meaningful gaze
Which leaves the receiver stunned and the giver in a maze

Of indeterminable doubt. Love has to be requited
For lovers, the world o'er, cannot fail to be excited

When each lives for the other. If two hearts beat as one
It is easy to imagine that you're somebody's 'Don Juan'.

And so I send this message. Receive it loud and clear.
"My love for you increases with every passing year.

Forget Romeo and Juliet; Harlequin and Columbine;
I have only one true love, and it's YOU, my Valentine!"

Love in the Afternoon

I think of you each second that you're away from me
And I even count the minutes 'cause I miss your company

Instinctively, like a zombie, I set about the chores
But my heart is just not in it and I often have to pause

To try to recall your last words before you went away
And although I pleaded with you I could not make you stay.

The time passes so slowly when your loved one is not there.
How often do I find myself glancing at his empty chair?

I cannot bear the waiting, it is driving me berserk.
Without him I can never concentrate upon my work.

I gaze out of the window but without real expectation
And until he reappears I am left in isolation.

Why can't I act more normally, as I did before we wed,
And banish him from all my thoughts? I ought to, but instead

I pace the floor and then sit down, a frown upon my face.
Why do I dwell upon the fact he's missing from this place?

A sideways glance at the mantel clock tells me I ought to start
On tidying up myself for I used to be so smart

And delighted in the many hours I spent getting ready
For a date with my dear 'boyfriend', before we started going steady.

Now, as newly-weds of a few months, we should be quite content
To love, honour and cherish was always our intent.

I told him not to leave but he didn't seem to hear me
And he doesn't understand how I need to have him near me.

So I'll pull myself together, count my blessings one by one
And, suddenly, my apprehension lifts and my gloom is gone.

A new spirit has come over me and I feel fighting fit.
I'll snap out of my lethargy, I am too young to quit

The game of life. After all he does enjoy the camaraderie
And, when the match is over he'll be back home for his tea!

A Moving Experience

There's a sign outside our house which says: 'This house for sale'.
I asked my mummy what it meant and she went rather pale.
"We're going to go away" she said "to start our life anew."
Through tears I pleaded "Please, mummy, may I come too?"

"Of course, my little cherub, we wouldn't leave you here.
No one else would want you, so you need have no fear.
And when we get a buyer to take this house off our hands
We'll buy ourselves a bungalow close to the golden sands."

I think that perhaps my mummy is being 'economical with the truth'
And my daddy is behaving like a 'bear with a sore tooth'.
He'd visited the Estate Agent and that's why he was late
Which sounds to me as if we'll finish up on an estate.

I heard him tell my mummy, as he drank another beer,
That he did not think the housing market would pick up this year.
I've been to Saturday markets, held on the market square,
But it must be a whopping market if they sell houses there!

Some strangers came today and they brought their little daughter,
She looked all around my bedroom and I don't think she ought-er
'Cause my bedroom is private and I keep my secrets there.
I wish she'd take her beady eyes off my old teddy bear.

We've sold the house and everything's on the removal van
And I think my darling daddy is a very clever man.
He's not only a teacher and sometimes plays the clown
But he's got himself a teaching post in a seaside holiday town.

I'm sorry to be leaving all the friends I've known for years
And I must confess it will be hard to hold back all my tears.
But I'm really looking forward to my home in Ullapool.
Yet sadly, even in Scotland, I still have to attend school!

Relatively Speaking

Why is it when you marry that the parents of your spouse
Tend to change their attitude to raging bull from timid mouse?
It's as if, previously, they dare not hint they were unkind
Lest you should break off this engagement and another fiancée find.

It is said that a daughter often becomes a double of her mother
And, for an innocent male, that could be a sign of potential bother.
So it is in a mother-in law's interest to be all sweetness and light
And then the future son-in-law is more likely his troth to plight.

But when the 'die is cast' and the newlyweds have tied the knot
It is then you begin to learn the kind of in-laws you have got.
Each time they make a visit, if an argument ensues,
You can bet they back their own child and you're the one to lose.

The in-laws are a special breed who think that they know best
Just because you were the one who plucked their youngest from the nest.
You don't really mind them coming and you love to see them go
But it's the period in between which irritates you so.

Your ways are always different when compared with the in-laws!
They'd never go down to the pub, when there is work to do indoors.
Although you've been on overtime throughout the month of June
You shouldn't leave your wife for rugby every Saturday afternoon.

Your wife may be a career girl and humour her boss for promotion
But should you stay late with female staff there will surely be commotion.
What's sauce for the gander may be relish for the goose
For the in-laws never trust a man when he is 'on the loose'.

But there is one thing about in-laws which is true throughout the land
If you really are in trouble they will always lend a hand.
It is only when you realise that in-laws aren't all that bad
And from being an interloper you become the son they never had.

Anxiety Is in the Mind of the Beholder

You say that you're not nervous, my young daughter,
Although A levels will come today
Your hard work this last year means that you ought t'
Obtain 'A's as grades, so why so much dismay?

As you sit there, apparently void of all emotion,
I guess your thoughts aren't really at their ease.
Look at it philosophically, that's my notion.
For your exam efforts should ensure some 'B's.

I know that it's a trying time and what is on your mind
But silence I would trade for your tirades
Of tantrums, moods and tears, if so inclined.
They are still passes if you get 'C' grades.

Why not get upon your feet and take some fresh air?
Even 'D' grades deserve a lot of praise my dear.
You say that you're not nervous and haven't got a care
So let's be optimistic… cast off your fear.

'E' grades don't mean you are past redemption
And I'm sure that grades alone won't make you quit
Another year of study will not cause contemption
So reconcile yourself for the resit.

But we cannot face the facts without the knowledge.
Hark! Is not that the letterbox, my dear?
I hope there is a letter from the college
Bringing the kind of news you want to hear.

Well, tell me the news, don't keep me waiting!
Though I know by your eyes you're all aglow.
You've got three 'A's! But that's a top rating!
My dear, did I not tell you so?

8: War

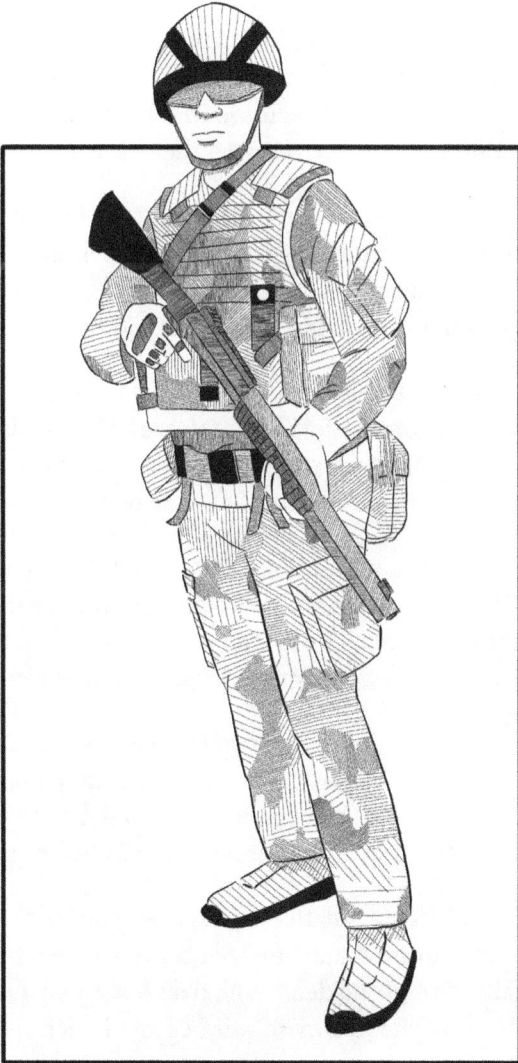

War... A Conflict as Much Mental as Physical

The prologue to war, disguised by patriotic euphoria,
Oft encompasses beliefs that battles will be short
And victory assured. So was it with the First World War
When rational sensibilities submerged beneath optimistic thought.

To be home by Christmas was the firm belief of those
Who the king's shilling took for freedom to maintain.
Yet four long years elapsed in 'Flanders Fields'
Before armistice restored the peace again.

The war itself soon produced stark reality
With thousands dying daily from the onslaught.
Those who survived the first bloody encounters
Their senses dimmed and nerves with fear were fraught.

Fear that the Allies would not be victorious.
Fear that one's effort might prove to be in vain
Fear that in the hour of need inadequacies may show.
Fear that their homeland they may never see again.

Afraid that if, with pals, they became too friendly
The shock of loss would be too hard to bear.
Afraid that loved ones would be left uncared for
And words of 'love unspoken' they might never hear.

Disturbed, their future seemed unsure and vulnerable.
Disturbed, that trench warfare they could not comprehend.
Disturbed, that they felt unequal to the conflict.
Disturbed, that they might prove cowards before the end.

War's aftermath is seen as anticlimax
After immediate, but brief, euphoric relief.
Realisation of the death toll, lives lost to no avail,
And the futility of war beggars belief.

Thoughts from the Trenches

Battleground trenches …
Despair, desolation,
Proximity, loneliness,
Fear, isolation.
Boredom and squalor,
Earth rent asunder.
Incessant noise
As the guns thunder.
Monotonous proximity
Of shock and shell,
Mud-splattered blasts,
Sharp showers of shrapnel.
Knee-deep in sludge,
Submerged duck-boards.
Barbed-wire barricades,
Rats by the hordes.
Numbness prevails
Over clarity of senses.
Sights sounds and smells
Which the brain condenses.
Each new day is dreaded,
There is no respite.
Only sheer fatigue
Allows sleep at night.
Soaked to the skin.
Miserable and cold.
The priority is …
To live to grow old!

Siegfried Sassoon, the War Poet

Siegfried Sassoon reveals to us all
the misery of the trenches.
In, truth, his rage of
disenchantment quenches
Everyone's desire to understand
the soldiers' plight

Great War, indeed! So many
slaughtered in the fight!
Filth, moral degradation,
decomposing corpses' stench,
Rats, terror and bewilderment,
submerged in a trench.

In satirising the 'brass hats'
and their apparent unconcern
Even to the futility of their
military operations, we learn
Decidedly that for those in authority,
war was beyond their ken.

Swore politicians "War won't end for at least
two years, but we've got stacks of men."
As a soldier, he wrote, joining
up on the very first day.
Sassoon won the Military Cross
during the Somme offensive, later throwing it away.

Severely wounded twice
in the furnace of the fighting,
Owen (Wilfred) claimed his trench life 'sketches'
were simply unique writing.
On hearing of the 'war jokes'
by which civilian consciences were assuaged

Newspapers' colourless phrases
needed him to set the honest stage.
The pen of Siegfried Sassoon
provided disenchantment for the mind,
His language hard and clear
but very sharply defined,

Expressing a mood of anti-heroic revolt
with such fervour and harsh wit
With questions: "Do they Matter? ...
Those dreams from the pit?"
A poet releasing emotions
far too deep to sever.

Recruits seen as 'too young to
fall asleep forever'.
Portraits of war, depicted by Sassoon
saw a war, at best,
Of defence and liberation
change to aggression and conquest.

Experience shone through a technique,
initially impulsive and raw
To recount to those at home
realistic truths about trench war.

Heroes All

We are an island nation
Surrounded by the sea
But we need to look beyond our shores
To attain our destiny.
Global actions do affect us
Be they political or economic
And, on a personal level,
Religious, racial and despotic.
It is then we come into our own
As a nation that does care
And, together with monetary aid,
If there's a need we're there.
Our brave efficient forces
In the air, on land and sea
Are sent to all parts of the world
Securing democracy.
To help beleaguered masses
Who suffer from oppression
Troops carrying out political policy
Deserve every one's compassion.
The forces who serve our country
Are alert for the global call.
Whatever the nature of the need
They are certainly 'heroes' all.

We should all recognise their efforts
When they venture to foreign lands
And pay them respect when they return
And be ready to shake their hands.
But in any confrontation
Sacrifices oft are made.
To the injured and those who gave their lives
Due honour must be paid.
There is only one way this can be done
Being cognisant of the families left.
The mothers, wives, brothers, sisters, daughters and sons
Need help when they are bereft.
The answer is simply 'Help for Heroes',
A charity for deserving forces
Who gave their lives for freedom's sake.
It supersedes all other causes.
With heroes to defend our shores
From cyber threats to terrorists' bands
Our 'land of hope and glory'
Is most certainly in safe hands.

Past Perfect

We may class ourselves as British but it really is a sin
If we do not always recognise our race's origin
From Angles, Saxons, Jutes and even Norman sources.
We, as a nation, owe it to a mixture of such forces.

After William conquered England he 'put paid' to more invasion
And, although many have tried, there has been no new occasion
When plunderers have struck or rampant hordes have stayed
Within our island shores which have repelled each raid.

Although Drake was preoccupied when the Great Armada came
And the Spaniards sailed around Britain yet the outcome was the same.
They never landed on our shores, though they had prepared well,
And many a British sailor had a victorious tale to tell.

Even Charles Stuart, when he came to claim the throne,
Found that Cumberland's resistance was a hard as stone
And, although Scottish supporters proved fanatically loyal,
The battle of Culloden was the last fought on British Soil.

Napoleon's flotilla was assembled, ready to attack the Brits,
But it was the British navy which made him 'call it quits.'
It was now left to the Duke of Wellington and the Prussians too
And it was in Belgium the French met their Waterloo.

But Hitler thought he'd won the war in the nineteen-forties
As he sent the German Luftwaffe on British airspace sorties.
But Britain, undismayed, sent into the sky lots
Of versatile spitfires and 'Battle of Britain' pilots.

So our fortress has remained intact more than nine hundred and fifty years
Achieve by honest toil and sweat and even blood and tears.
But let our erstwhile vigilance remain and never cease
Lest our sovereignty, retained in war, is stolen in the peace.

9: Every Place Has Its Unique Appeal

WELCOME TO SCARBOROUGH

Britain's First Resort

Yorkshire's Warmest Welcome

Filey

There's a place I'd love to live,
in the North-East, by the sea
Where the air is always clear
and one's thoughts are fancy-free.
It's my preferred resort
which is thought of very highly
And this Cote D'Azur of the English coast
is simply known as Filey.

To holiday at Filey
one does not have to be too wealthy
And as one breathes the briny air
one immediately feels more healthy
Of all the English resorts
it is the least commercialised
And provides the idyllic charm
over which folk fantasised.

The reality is that Filey,
as a resort, is simply grand
With sea and sun and fishing boats
as well as golden sand.
The position of the crescent, overlooking the sea,
is most commanding
But should you wish to traverse the beach
there's none better than Coble Landing.

There ample children's play areas
so very close at hand
But nothing on a sunny day
beats buckets, spades and sand.
Yet those for whom just idleness
and watching the sea, palls
There is handy light refreshment
from the numerous sea food stalls.

Filey folk are friendly
and you don't feel you're a stranger
And while bathing in the bay
there is scarcely any danger.
If relaxation is your quest
you could do a lot worse
And I promise you that it will not
completely drain your purse.

One can gaze through water
crystal clear onto the flat sea-bed
Or journey north to Bempton Cliffs
or south to Flamborough Head.
At Bempton you'll see razorbills,
puffins and gannets nesting
And a brisk walk between Flamborough Landings
should not prove too testing.

As you view the rugged coastline
you will want to call it 'home'
Never more you'll get the urge
which makes you want to roam.
Whatever you have been in life
if you really love the sea
You'll easily settle on the coast
in the town they call Filey.

Memories of Filey

Filey Bay
Sunny Day
Seafood Stalls
Raucous Calls
Coble Landing
Gulls Demanding
Tasty Snacks
From Fishing Smacks
Sandy Beach
Within Reach
Sea and Sand
A Brass Band
In Demand
Raised Bandstand
Sailing Yachts
Guillemots
Victorian Fete
Animal Date
Lifeboat Crew
Panoramic View
Buoys and Gulls
Squalls and Lulls
Filey Brig
Never Infra dig

A Village... Past and Present

The thatch has long gone
Replaced by slate or pantile
But some cottages remain
In a modernised style.
Delightful views across the Trent
With low ground and high.
Shipbuilding and ferry are now defunct
But lorries to the wharf still go by.
The Church and the Methodist Chapel
Provide solace for religious souls.
There are activities for all age groups
With a children's play area and a green for bowls.
At the approach to the village
A windmill once ground corn for the farms.
The original Black Bull Inn
Has been named the Sheffield Arms.
Indoor events are catered for
In the Todd's Lane Village Hall
And the Westland's Social Club
Extends a warm welcome to all.
The above describes a delightful place
And those who inhabit it will gather
I refer to the village where I reside
Named Burton-upon-Stather.

Burton-upon-Stather... A Tribute

Before it won its accolade of 'Best Kept Village' title
The residents of Burton knew their village was supreme.
For a village to be special one ingredient is vital,
The populace must be prepared to work as a good team.

The shopkeepers and local pubs have a huge part to play
With a cheerful greeting and a friendly smile.
It helps the weary customer to get through the day
Making one feel special and not just 'rank and file'.

Facilities in the village cater for young and old
With a playing field for youngsters and a seniors' bowling green
Where the members share the upkeep without being told
To do so. It is all part of the co-operative scene.

There's a social club which welcomes all to many facilities
And the village hall is open so village groups can meet.
Burton certainly caters for all ages and abilities
And helps to keep the bored from congregating on the street.

Burton boasts an ancient Church and a newer Methodist Hall
Which give spiritual succour to those in need.
A surgery provides all one's medical advice on call
And the village is self-sufficient, oh yes indeed.

But I hear you say "What does Burton possess
Which other villages cannot emulate?"
Its setting in the natural landscape is my answer, I guess,
For the view from Burton Heights is simply great.

The approaches to the village suggest it is well kept
Especially when the daffodils are blooming.
At maintaining short grass verges, villagers are adept
And their efforts in this regard are unassuming.

The village boasts a scenic route which many ramblers walk
And there's a panoramic view to feat one's eyes on.
Locals do say, that on a clear day, they can see as far as York
And the Minster can be seen on the horizon.

The river Trent flows slowly past Burton's lower reaches
Though there's no material evidence of the once-used ferry.
Yet it features in accounts that many a historian teaches
And the Ferry House Inn retains the name for history.

Burton residents all work towards a common goal
And taking part gives one a 'special kick'.
The organising committees take a vital role
And community involvement does the trick.

During the recent lockdown, due to Coronavirus,
The willingness to help the vulnerable shows goodwill.
I am sure that urban communities certainly must admire us
In shopping for the elderly, the disabled and the ill.

So thank you to the residents for springing to the cause
In the unprecedented times we all endure.
It saves the aged and disabled from visiting the stores
And surely we who benefit could hardly ask for more.

The Town of Gainsborough

I was born in the county of Lincolnshire's
Market town of Gainsborough
Where the local books of history recount
That 'Yellow Bellies' fear no foe.
The town featured in Eliot's 'Mill on the Floss'
As a thriving river port
But, erstwhile, in the region of Cavendish Bog
Many a Civil War battle was fought.
There's a manor house built for a lord of the land
Called 'The old Hall' from Tudor times
And the area has countless tales to tell
From Lea Marshes to Morton 'Gymes'.
When a network of mediaeval dwellings was built
The town had its moment of fame
For the artisans built only on the high lands
Which was spared when the flood waters came.
Allowing egress to the North and North East
The Trent Bridge was conveniently placed
But it is to the birth of steam traction, I think,
That the town's wealth can really be traced.
As well as the old LMS railway line
We were served by the LNER
Which introduced engineers to the town
And links with places afar.
In an age when manpower was prosperity's key
The workforce fed Marshall's and Rose's
But with the advent of computerised skills
It's small towns like Gainsborough which loses.
Service industries now provide most of the jobs
Heavy industry is out in the cold
But before we toll Gainsborough's final death knell
Let's delight... in its glories of old

Scarborough

The resurgent sun arises from eastern horizons
Through a hazy sea mist heralding a new day.
Sea birds' raucous chorus welcoming the dawning
And waves gently ripple into the north and south bay.

The streaky blue sky, with its high wispy clouds,
Is reflected in the sea but with a stronger hue,
The temperature's rising and there is a stillness
And the whole panorama's like a postcard view.

In the mid-eighties Fahrenheit even with the sea breezes,
Surely summer has come to our shores at long last
And whether it remains for one day or longer,
It recalls the hot summers we enjoyed in the past.

It is on days like this that folk flock to Scarborough,
The queen of resorts on Yorkshire's East Coast.
It's treasured by those who choose it for holidays
But those who reside there appreciate it the most.

10: Crime

A Knock on the Door

Blackmail: extortion with menaces,
The vilest crime when, as is
The custom, to succumb to pressures
Is inevitably the precursor to further measures.
Yet, to take a stance and demands ignore
What are you letting yourself in for?

When the knock came on the door
I was expecting it, for sure
Though that did nothing to assuage my apprehension
My pounding heart did raise my hypertension.

The two stood there in aggressive mode
While I felt vulnerable as a land-locked toad.
The younger of the two was the spokesman
And words came smoothly, as was the plan,
To leave the victim in no doubt
As to what their mission was about.
It was a 'demand' rather than an 'ask'
Enhanced by the grimace on the Hallowe'en mask.
The dreaded words, far from discreet,
Were, 'Hello Mister! Trick or Treat?'

The Crime of One's Life

Crime has always been with mankind
ever since life appeared earth
And whether the cause is genetic
or acquired after birth
Is a question over which
the various pundits disagree
But it may be inequalities in life
which hold for us the key.

If the genes are to blamed
for a person's life of crime
It may explain those poverty-stricken
through generations of time.
'Like father, like son'
used to be a favourite saying,
Crime being the only way
to keep the 'door wolf' from baying.

But if one mixes from an early age
with the criminal fraternity
One can emulate their deeds of crime
to seek fame for eternity.
For greed is not only acquiring
material possessions as mere wealth
But, also, can be kudos gained
by the 'adrenalin' of stealth.

Crime will never be eliminated
as humans are not programmed
To follow virtuous lives because
their brains are also crammed
With conflicting information.
Some lives are adulterated while others may be pure
And crime will never be preventable
and we'll never find a cure.

As to whether twenties crime is worse
cannot be revealed
For we live in different times.
it's not a 'level playing field'.
Not only have the police
sophisticated aids to detect crimes
But the criminals have technological skills
not possessed in former times.

Greed, Jealousy, envy and power
have always driven men's ambitions
And if fair means don't satisfy those cravings
one turns to other missions
To achieve one's goals in life.
Even those whose criminal thoughts are rare
May be betrayed by extreme frustration
and the feeling of despair.

I do not think that crime is worse
than it was in previous times
It's just that now the media relates
the details of all crimes.
Wherever you live in the world today
the coverage is international
So it is easy to become obsessed with crime
which is totally irrational.

Yet, should you be an unfortunate victim
of any sort of crime
You will certainly believe that crime has worsened
one hundred percent of the time.

11: The Sea

The Call of the Sea

It may be because Britain's an island,
Allied with its naval tradition,
That the British respond to the 'call of the sea'
Regardless of age or position.

The British, geographically speaking,
Are conveniently placed for the sea
And when annual holidays beckon
It is the one place to be.

During the thirties' Depression
When day trips were common by train
Parents took the holiday excursion to the seaside
To breathe the pure ozone again.

The exodus to coastal waters
Began before school days for most
And armed with a bucket and spade each
Parents took their 'bairns' to the coast.

At that age one's needs were quite simple
And the holiday had not to be planned.
You merely left what you were doing
To spend the whole day on the sand.

In one's teens one's tastes differed somewhat,
Not with parents, but alone with one's mates.
One set off for seaside amusements
And longed for those 'holiday dates'.

The sea still retained its fascination.
Football was oft played on the sand.
One might even go for a cruise around the bay
And that kiss 'neath the pier was just grand.

The call of the sea during wartime
Was answered by the young and the brave
But some never returned to tell the tale
Confined to a watery grave.

Those who survived turbulent war years
Are now of retirement age.
They oft wish to settle somewhere near the sea
In a bungalow, flat or cottage.

The emotions of man run parallel with
The ebb and the flow of the sea
Denoting placidity, calmness and peace
With a streak of natural cruelty!

So whether you've been a seafaring man
Or view the sea with some consternation
You must accept, that in spite of all else,
The sea has a unique fascination.

The Enigmatic Sea

Because we live on an island
our lives are controlled by the sea
Which acts as a natural defence
and provides some security.
Though separated from Europe's mainland,
isolation is far from the case
In an age when sea and air transport
unites the whole human race.

But the sea has an awesome power
which defies humans to outwit
And over the years brave seafaring men
have singularly failed to tame it.
There's been many a titanic struggle
waged between ships and the sea
And 'Davy Jones' Locker' gives witness
as to which gained final victory.

The calmness of the coastal oceans
reminds us of ducks on a lake
But the angry sea in a force ten gale
makes hardened seadogs quake.
It is a fight against superior elements,
manmade structures find hard to withstand,
And it's not so surprising, really,
that humans feel safest on land.

It's as if seas resent the intrusion of life
that is less than marine
And those who've not experienced one-hundred-feet waves
cannot really picture the scene.
Yet landlubbers know that wild seas
will provide all naval men with a duel
Each time they venture the oceans to cross.
How can the seas be so cruel?

To all of an island's people,
whatever their calling may be,
Geographically speaking, wherever they live,
it can't be too far from the sea.
They visit the coast regularly,
especially on annual vacation,
For whether you worship or fear it,
the sea has this strange fascination.

12: Nursing

Nurse-ry Rhyme

When admitted to a hospital what do we expect?
Certainly the nurses deserve your full respect.
Their devotion to duty, their care and thankless work
Are evidence that, however distasteful, no tasks do they shirk.

A nurse is a model of service and confidentiality
Dealing with all patients regardless of abnormality.
For erstwhile quiet humans develop demanding traits
And politeness is oft forgotten when illness predominates.

Nursing is a vocation and I've often heard it said:
"They don't enrol as nurses for the pittance they are paid."
A large pay award is needed for it is surely belated
And of all the professional posts nursing is most under-rated.

What really keeps the nurses sane is their wit and repartee
For, whatever the circumstances, good humour is the key.
Especially in the surgical ward some patients can be bitches
But nurses easily cope with this and soon everyone's in stitches!

When enquiring of a male patient for an update of condition
Nurses are always forthright and make a quick decision.
If his behaviour's normal then it means that he's not worse
But don't be too surprised if he takes a turn for the 'nurse'!

Emptying a patient's bedpan when confined to bed
Is a necessary chore which most new nurses dread
But when one has to administer the cleansing enema
Without the use of bedpans think of the alternative dilemma!

An elderly male patient to the nurse complained again
That hospitals had no spittoons for tobacco-chewing men.
"I miss those old spittoons" said he as he chewed on his quid.
The quick retort from the Staff Nurse was "yes, you always did!"

Nurses use initiative in every eventually.
They make quick decisions to avoid the slightest casualty.
One even bounced a patient on the bed at near full throttle
For she had taken her medicine but forgotten to shake the bottle!

What tales the nurses all could tell re the Wards on Level D
Especially surgical wards and wards used for maternity
Where labour may be caused by a Liberal-minded Tory
So they rush her up to Level E, but that's another storey!

Consultants need to explore inside one's digestive tract.
For this they use an endoscope, a rather delicate act.
It is like an all-seeing eye with yards of tube to follow.
And they provide an anaesthetic should it be hard to swallow.

A patient suffering from haemorrhoids, the pain she could not face,
Was told, in the 'back passage' the suppository to place.
The ward had no back passage and this patient was so dumb
That she placed it in the vestibule instead of in her b--!

Each year medical knowledge is advancing at great pace
But we still need the nursing service to be there face to face.
How soon will keyhole surgery solve problems of the womb?
And does it mean the surgeon will operate 'outside the room?'

I hope this poem of mine will not cause offence
For one's gratitude to nursing staff is really quite immense
And whereabouts you choose to travel in visiting foreign lands
We know that here in England patients are mainly in safe hands.

'Womb' Service

Six months age my GP diagnosed my womb had dropped.
It certainly disturbed me and 'in my tracks I stopped!'
I was referred to a consultant, confirmation was the aim
Then after cursory examination his diagnosis was the same.

The 'panic' nearly set in as operations aren't for me,
When I was told I would need a hysterectomy.
The only saving grace which made it easier to bear
Was that it would not happen for at least half a year.

As each month passed my blood pressure began to rise a little
And at last I was admitted to Scunthorpe General Hospital.
It was a bed in Ward 27 that my immediate 'home' would be
So I made my way along corridors and up to level D.

Well start with a good old enema the nurse explained, with glee,
It'll prepare you for the theatre and clean you thoroughly.
We'll then give you a clip down under and that will make your day
But you won't have a Yul Brynner, we must keep infection at bay.

I was given much assurance and made to feel a 'welcome guest'
And nurses, surgeon and anaesthetist all set my mind at rest.
Everyone was very helpful as I was made ready for my 'op'
And they said after recuperation, I would soon feel tiptop.

Dressed in my pure white stockings and my 'height of fashion' gown
They put me on a trolley and slowly pushed ne down
The long, unending corridors until I reached the theatre
Where, on this operating stage, I was to be the 'main feature'.

The next thing I remember was awakening from a dream.
The time was nearly six o'clock and, strange as it may seem,
My head was floating in the clouds, a numbness pervaded me
And soon my eyes were closed again and I felt serenity.

The following day feeling 'over the moon' I was up and raring to go
And amazed to find how well I felt but little did I know
That pain-killing injections and my anaesthetic state
Would not last forever and my euphoria would abate.

My 'lesson' has been learnt and I'm now more 'on my mettle'
I believe those who warned me it would be hard to lift a kettle.
I must not stretch or bend quickly and I cannot carry weights
I have to do as I am told, relying heavily on my mates.

But thanks to devoted nursing care and a staff nurse who understands
I have returned home determined to limit household demands.
The work will have to wait until my convalescence ends
And it is now I need the support of helpful faithful friends.

13: Seasons

Easter Acknowledges Spring, Trumpeting Earth's Renewal

Each twelve months has four seasons which govern our lives
And delighted I feel when the spring season arrives.
My fond love of the spring has multifarious reasons
Which don't apply in the same way to the other three seasons.

For spring-time is the start of the seasonal year
Bringing with it all things that my heart holds so dear.
I'm able to relegate to the back of my mind
The cold winter months which can be so unkind.

Spring sees the awakening of aconites and snowdrops,
For spring flowers are the daintiest of all the bulb crops,
And the lengthening of the day suggests nature unlocks
The best of all seasons at the vernal equinox.

The dark clouds are less frequent and the sky a rich blue
And without mist and fog one can admire the view.
The air is quite warm and the sun rises early.
There may be some rain but snowstorms are seen rarely.

The birds begin nesting and young lambs appear
And everyone you meet is full of good cheer
Scented blossoms soon abound, hibernators awake
And delicious foliage grows after the winter break.

Lent leads us into Easter, with the Resurrection,
Both Jesus' rebirth and nature's renewal are viewed with affection.
Of all the religious festivals, Easter is the jewel.
Easter Acknowledges Spring Trumpeting Earth's Renewal.

Spring, to me, epitomises a new start on this earth
When all God's creatures experience the thrill of rebirth
And, as it happens annually, we need have no fear
For with God's good grace we'll enjoy the same next year.

Springtime... An Alternative View

Spring brings with it the promise
of better days to come
Yet its March opening is early and,
alas there may be some
Of the less acceptable traits of winter
which still linger on,
Although the temperature may rise
when blessed with early morning sun.

Life in early spring
can be a harsh and buffeting time.
There is poverty in the landscape
and a bleakness, less sublime
Than the seasonal experts suggest.
Winter's cold and dark
Has meant growth has been suspended
and all plant life is stark.

Thus, spring is at the lowest point
of the year, gales often at their fiercest
And between the sun's rise and setting
the temperature difference is at its steepest.
The moisture from the oceans
has filled the rivers and the streams
And there's a lull of expectation,
or that is how it seems.

The current that propels the tide
is on its strongest run
When the earth's elliptical orbit
comes nearest to the sun,
Preparing for the light and the warmth
of which summer days are full
Until plant and animal life do grow,
there's bound to be a lull.

Heavily, we rely on nature's
hierarchy of oscillations
With their equinoctial high tides
and all their machinations.
Although man 'puts the clocks forward'
to encourage the seasonal race
Spring has its own internal clock
and arrives at its own pace.

So spring hasn't necessarily arrived
with the first primrose
For frost, or even snow,
in April can certainly impose.
A curb on man's belief
that a new season is dawning.
Spring needs a few weeks' grace
to dissipate last winter's awning.

14: Miscellany

The 'A's Have It

With reminiscent past life one can appreciate one's schooldays
And, with the spur of competition, how one worked to achieve 'A's
In all subjects. For an 'A' was a mark of excellence
And to a parent, any lower grade was a sign of indolence.
As life progressed, assessment came and 'A' was the preferred notion
Which kept one in the forefront and in line for swift promotion.
But top grades became commonplace, with most scholars studious,
And ambition fostered a new grade known simply as 'A plus'.
Achievement led to higher rungs reached on ones ladder of success
With additional bank deposits available for material excess.
It is when one has security that one purchases a house and a car
And then the two 'A's may appear to assist one from afar.
One signs up with the two 'A's without a minute's hesitation
For it's wise to cover all mishaps with the Automobile Association
But should a penchant for drink become one's Achilles heel
Then, perhaps, to Alcoholics Anonymous one may have to make appeal.
But don't neglect the three 'A's as one begins to accrue wealth
For the Amateur Athletics Association maintains fitness for one's health.
And if one adds Acceptance to Ambition and Achievement,
Those three 'A's will sustain us from conceivement to bereavement.

Out of Sight, out of Mind

Why is it that Englishmen, so meek and mild at home,
Suddenly become aggressive… in Paris, Bonn or Rome?
Why does the Englishman's blood pressure begin to rise
Immediately you let him loose beneath the foreign skies?

There may be several reasons which cause this transformation
To make the most subservient guy act below his station.
So I'll suggest some reasons why he becomes outrageous
And why the English find adverse behaviour so contagious.

Because the Latins and the Franks have 'the lovers' reputation
When it comes to emulation, Englishmen need inspiration
Which seems part of every package deal compiled by travel clubs
For there's more than just 'Dutch Courage' to be obtained from foreign pubs.

In England men's professional standing controls how they perform
But in a land where they are strangers, heavy drinking becomes the norm.
Excess liquor leads to drunkenness which makes them easy prey
To the pressures of the peer group for vices prevalent today.

It used to be in days long gone, when Englishmen went abroad
They took with them idiosyncrasies, as foreign parts were explored.
That's why the impression of Englishmen, by all the various races,
Was one of rolled-up trousers, cloth cap and elastic braces.

But those days have now passed and they venture further from their home
As they adopt the well-known maxim beginning "When in Rome…"
Which seems to inflame their passions and deprive them of common sense
As they gleefully indulge in drinking, sex and perhaps violence.

But Englishmen venture abroad on other occasions, it seems,
That is when there are football games involving English teams.
It is then that national pride is often tested to the full
And an erstwhile loyal supporter can become a raging bull!

Or is it due to history that we dislike the foreigner so
And feel that every European, at one time, has been our foe?
So when the German claims the last remaining deckchair near the pool
We remember the last two great wars and our anger they do fuel.

The French may be close neighbours but we've rarely been close friends
But with the Channel Tunnel surely our isolation ends,
We crave a universal language and we think it would be good
If everyone spoke English then we would be understood.

So, as Englishmen, we go abroad for annual holidays.
It's the best chance we really have of enjoying the sun's rays.
The food is good, hotels are cheap and so they are the gainers
But, unfortunately, in English eyes, the natives are foreigners!

The Proverbial Grindstone

In the steel-making town of Scunthorpe
we have our bungalow
And when they are tapping the furnaces
we can see the rosy glow.
But if one earns his or her living
in a town some miles away
One has to develop a daily routine
for every working day.

It's worse during the season of winter,
especially when there is snow
Because the roads then can be treacherous,
as all commuters know.
It's dark when one awakens
with the sleep still in one's eyes
And it's dark when one arrives home…
oh how the daytime flies.

From the moment one arrives at work
the problems come thick and fast
And when you think you've dealt with them
and the worst ones surely have passed
It is then a major crisis into your in-tray drops
For it's when the pressure mounts
you learn where the real buck stops.

To be classed as executive staff may be regarded as a perk
But white-collared workers invariably
are those always involved in 'homework'
And should they stay late at the office
to complete the work of the day
No financial inducement is given
in the form of overtime pay.

The way remuneration is paid for work
is where another controversy rages
For professionals are usually paid salaries
while manual workers receive wages.
Wages are paid weekly
which means fifty-two payments each year
But salaried staff receive twelve monthly cheques,
leaving them four weeks in arrear!

Solely on the manager's shoulders
responsibility rests like a weight
And it's not really surprising
that the pressure exerted is great.
The older one gets, reaction is slower
and defence against criticism less.
If this continues for a month after month
it becomes manifested as stress.

Work may be a nuisance which one can't avoid
in keeping the 'wolves from the door'
And when it takes over to such a degree
that one's social life is no more
It's time to sit down, reflect on one's role
and decide what is really desired.
The one saving grace, in my own case,
I'm thankful that I have retired!

Is It a Game... Or Is It War?

Of all the games of skill there are few rivals to chess
Wherein the top-class players achieve a worldwide fame
Tactics and basic strategies, combined with some finesse,
Suggest that, at this level, it's the ultimate war game.

The battlefield's a chequered board, set out as a square,
With divisions coloured alternatively black and white.
The different pieces on the board reminiscent of 'la guerre'
Each have a unique movement when employed in the 'fight'.

The King piece is the leader to be guarded at all cost.
Limited mobility ensures it's kept from the front line.
Should your king be cornered then the whole war is lost
For a leaderless militia means the one course is 'Resign!'

Behind every successful male a female oft appears.
In the game of chess the Queen supplies the guile.
She is the piece most mobile and the 'Ship of State' she steers
As she protects the King's board-life and attacks in her own style.

Knights represent the cavalry as they into battle go
Aided in their sorties by their unique means of 'taking'
Such rare flexibility provides danger to the foe
And should they jeopardise themselves its oft of their own making.

All wars bring out in man a latent religious bent
And in chess, as in life, there's no exception
Where Bishops provide a necessary spiritual element
And an attacking force in diagonal direction.

Castles epitomise the ramparts behind which the King can wait
And the act of 'castle-ing' is to strengthen his defence.
Castles move either forward or sideways, provided they go straight,
Which makes the defeat of the King a task immense.

As in wars, the lives of infantry are the lowest priced,
In chess the Pawns are given this thankless role.
In early exchanges on the board Pawns are sacrificed
As strategic use of pieces takes its toll.

If sufficient secure protection for the King one can't provide
His vulnerability keeps him in 'check' or on the run
And finally, when this piece has nowhere left to hide
'Checkmate' then means the war game has been won.

Chess sets come in various sizes but most are modelled well
As befits a game of attack and doux defence.
About many a well-won battle the chequered board can tell
Yet, stalemate can also be the consequence.

Fair Comment

Each Easter saw the annual fair
appear on the green
And you were thought an outcast
if you could not say you'd been
To spend your money freely
on sideshows, sweets and rides.
There was barrel-organ music,
flashing lights and more besides.

You usually went to the fairground
with a group of friends
Determined to enjoy yourselves,
especially at weekends.
Joy and fear combined,
culminating in loud screams,
And the roller coaster ride
was beyond your wildest dreams.

But rides were not cheap options,
even in those days,
So to eke out pocket money
there were several other ways
Of enjoying yourselves.
The attractive sideshows were varied and many
With rifle range, coconut shy,
hoop-la and roll-a-penny.

The rifles at the rifle range
were rarely accurate enough
And you knew to win a prize
that the going would be tough.
Your first shot was a marker,
telling you about the sight,
So you could adjust your next shots,
firing to the left or to the right.

To knock a coconut completely
out of its sandy nest
You had to hit it at least twice
with considerable zest.
The firmly seated coconut
had to be disturbed with your first hit
And, hopefully, the second
would dislodge it from its 'pit'.

Even if you ringed the hoop-la prize
you hardly ever ringed the block.
No wonder that from year to year
they retained the same old stock.
But to win at roll-a-penny
was a skill so quickly learned
You simply placed the coins on the board
when the assistant's back was turned!

To satisfy your taste buds,
as you munched beneath the stars,
You could always buy pink and white
nutty nougat bars.
But the day had to come
when the fair packed and went
Leaving you fond memories
until next year's event.

Communication... A Gift to Treasure

It is said that it is better to give than to receive
And it's a wise saw if that giving should momentarily relieve
One's suffering or heartache. But gifts don't have to be
Merely of the material kind. Words and actions hold the key.

A friendly greeting, with a smile, will oft uplift
A depressed spirit. Undoubtedly, the gift
Of friendship, oft undervalued by the donor,
Is appreciated by all but even more by a 'loner'.

A meaningful wave or a squeeze of the hand
Brings a feeling of warmth which all can understand.
But to stop for a word and a brief one will do,
Can rekindle one's worth and confidence renew.

To call on a neighbour, to check on the health
Of an aged senior citizen, is prized more than wealth.
To someone alone what pleasure it brings
When, quite unexpectedly, the telephone rings.

A letter or card with appropriate greeting
Or a walk down the street and a chance meeting
With someone prepared to listen with interest
Provide pleasant divergence for the lonely and depressed.

Delivered flowers and chocolates can be a surprise.
They will be most welcome and bring tears to the eyes
Of the recipient. But personal delivery beats sending by post.
It's the visit, not the present, which is valued the most.

So remember, when you have a few minutes to spare
That a friendly stranger is somewhere out there.
Brighten his or her day with a smile and a word
And, unlike a small child, be both 'seen and heard'.

Time Management

To those who find that time is scarce
Who panic and get stressful
It surely makes the problem worse,
As one can't be successful
When coping with the teasing thought
That time is insufficient.
Yet, efforts only come to nought,
Despite the person's good intent,
Where care outweighs thought's clarity.
Cure! It lies in management
Of time as a necessity.
Those who see that time is spent
In organising relevant
Arrangements, before too late,
Will thus avoid the critic's chant:
"Never dare procrastinate".
No one is indispensable
Because one day, without a doubt,
However unpalatable,
The sands of time do run out!

And You Thought You Had Problems

When we speak of hunger it is relatively speaking
For it's only three hours since breakfast and it's lunch we are seeking
But for those for whom a square meal is something they never see,
Hunger pangs are not just fleeting but a permanent legacy.

If you cut your hand or gash your head or tread on a drawing-pin
It is easy to complain, moan, groan and make a raucous din
But when compared with loss of limb or even loss of sight
You realise that your minor ills are no measure for others' plight.

You may not like it very much when caught in wind and rain
But at least, with modern heating, you can soon get dry again.
Not so the countless homeless folk who sleep rough in all weather.
Don't tell them that one rainy day is the extent of your tether.

Please control your temper when your car ignition fails
Or you have a tyre blow-out on a journey to the Dales.
Those mishaps are part of life which increased technology brought.
Far worse when 'shank's pony' is your sole means of transport.

When faced with a full wardrobe one deliberates on what to wear
But not so countless poor people who face life with just despair.
For them no 'Sunday Best' a smart suit or shimmering gown
As what they stand up and sleep in is all the clothes they own.

One reads of affluent people whose foreign holiday ends in tears
But it's not headline news if holidays are unaffordable for years
And the next time you start boasting of the bargains you have bought
Just spare a little thought for those on family income support.

Next time the dog shakes himself and with mud the hall wall it spatters
Remember a wipe erases it so, long term, it hardly matters.
But if your home's a cardboard box you have no hall at all
And you're thankful to erect your box near any mud-stained wall.

Patronymics and Other Derivations

Before surnames were used, Christian names identified
The locals, in small settlements, and their needs were satisfied.
But as civilisation advanced and populations began to rise
Surnames were needed urgently, individuals to recognise.

So, to avoid chaos which inertness would surely raise,
Surnames were obtained speedily in many different ways.
Some came from father's first name or where one had one's roots
While others described occupations or physical attributes.

Johnson is the son of John, keeping the name when he marries,
Harrison is the son of Harry or it could simply be Harris.
'Fitz', 'Mac' and 'O' prefixing names have relations filial
And provide us with Fitzpatrick, MacDonald and O' Dannall.

More surnames were obtained based on where one did reside
Producing Bridges, Moor and Hill; Dale, Marshland and Fieldside.
Some natural phenomena feature such as 'Well' 'Ford' and 'Burn',
At the end of people's surnames, making Newell, Bradford and Blackburn!

Some names come from regions such as North, South, West and East
While others favour villages, Laughton and Blyth not being the least.
Towns are not forgotten with York, Lancaster and Swannick.
Indeed, anywhere in Britain could have a patronymic.

Occupations, also, can denote ones 'Kin and Kith',
A woodworker would be a Wright and a metalworker, Smith.
Other obvious surnames based on work include the well-known Baker,
Archer, Barber, Cook and the very old Shoemaker.

Surnames also derive from appearance, habits dress or manner
So we get Little, Spendlove, Smart, Charmer or Chalmer.
But those called White, Grey, Black or even Redhead
Owe it to their hair colouring, or so I've heard it said.

So surnames evolved in various ways, as outlined in this verse,
But some may think that they have made the situation worse
For almost three per cent of the population has the common 'Smith' surname.
So do surnames really make it easier to achieve the desired aim?

Futurity

If I could foresee the future and my predictions were prophetic
I would search for fundamental changes as well as the aesthetic.
My view would be long- sighted rather than myopic
With an all-embracing focus that would be anastigmatic.

There will be significant change in the year two thousand twenty-three
Since Britain has withdrawn from what was once the EEC.
And our ties with the USA will lead to American Domination
As we finally accept our role as third-rate nation.

The House of Lords will soon be gone with the Commons' power less
As we rely for our finances on the American Congress.
With inflation soaring and unemployment an all-time high
We will mourn the decline of industry and ask the question "Why?"

Fifty years from now I predict England without royalty
And to a Republican President we'll have to pledge our loyalty.
The once-regal English palaces will have become anachronistic
And turned into museums for those remaining royalistic.

With a paucity of sporting skills 'beggars can't be choosers'
As Britain retains its reputation for being 'jolly good losers'
Reports on the tiddlywinks championship at Wembley will be succinct,
The erstwhile British champion having tiddled instead of winked!

Since the 1990s' BSE crisis, no more cows will have been bred
So the consumer will have to rely for milk on the herds of goats instead.
The shortage of fish will mean few fish-and-chip shops will remain
And this traditional dish, frozen, will be imported from Spain!

Conservationists will defeat the planners regarding new highways.
Carpets of wild flowers will reappear on most rural byways.
The birds will find hedgerows again where they can safely nest
And environmentalists will have triumphed in their incessant quest.

My predictions in the main, have a pessimistic theme.
Let's be optimistic that they're not as bad as they first seem!

True Values

When we come into this world we have nothing.
All our gains are made while we are on this earth.
Although some of us may benefit more than others
Parental advantages determine our true worth.

But we should not let ourselves be avaricious
Or let material accumulation be our goal
For it's personal possessions which cause envy, greed and hate
And do nothing for the goodness of our soul.

Every human being deserves an education,
A free service which the State needs to uphold,
And although we need some money to live a happy life
We should not imitate the miser's love of gold.

To be envious of others causes heartache.
It means one is not too happy with one's lot.
Life's most prized gifts cannot be bought for money.
Good health's more precious that a luxury yacht.

It's better to give generously than receive as if by right
For amassing wealth rarely brings peace of mind.
Generosity and a caring heart reap their own reward
And it does not cost huge sums just to be kind.

Treat everyone as you would have them treat you.
Bear no grudge and banish preconceptions.
Should other's values differ from your own in any way
Still maintain your stand. Make no exceptions!

Simplicity of life and a leisurely approach
Are the goals that all fair-minded people seek.
Don't be led by crass ambition as you make your way through life
For it's true, "the Earth's inherited by the Meek".

What's in a Name?

When naming a child some parents have a real knack
And the stamp of approval goes to daughter Penny Black.

But who would be stupid enough, even if they dare,
To Christen one's daughter as plain Connie Fir?

With the surname Pending you can keep it for perpetuity,
Call your daughter Pat and leave it to inventor's ingenuity.

For a Christmas to be Mary one's perhaps scraping the barrel
But not so much a Mr Service calling his child Carol!

If your surname is Dover then it could be an ill-omen
That you will be mischievous if your parents call you Ben.

A person Christened Gaylord, if he is big and strong,
May be called Gay for short, though not for very long.

With my girlfriend, Gertrude, I thought I'd scored a hit
When she said "Call me Gert and leave off the rude bit!"

'Bill Stickers to be prosecuted' the timely warning went.
Some wag added to this notice. 'Bill Stickers innocent!'

The family Day if they choose May, as a rhyme to enthral,
Could find their daughter's name becomes a distress signal call.

With a surname Castle then the parents are surely to blame
If their son tends to be dated should Norman be his name.

Lord Vere made his choice and showed no filial mercy
Thinking more of the family motto when he named his son Percy.

Mark Time would be a soldier as it appears to me
And an Okie, named as Carrie, surely has to sing in key.

If Ono's daughter Kim suggests a cover-up at dawning
Then perhaps Nick O'Teen needs a Government health warning.

Jerry Mander's credentials demand a career in politics
While a field known as Paddy would use rice to get his kicks.

So before you Christen your child have a thought for him or her
Lest they have to go through life with a name they cannot bear.

Road Works

On the road where we live the road surface was in 'fine fettle'
Thanks to John MacAdam the tarmac was hard as metal.
There were no ruts, loose stones or potholes and the camber drained well
But for how long would it remain so? Time and providence would tell.

When works to be undertaken collaboration is unknown
For councils and public utilities have a work schedule of their own.
So when a new house was constructed on adjacent building land
All the usual public services soon appeared to lend a hand.

British Gas was the first workforce. They arrived in pouring rain.
They'd hoped to link the customer with the gas from the gas main.
Instead they spent the morning deliberating on the task,
Sheltering in their vehicle and drinking from their flask.

In the afternoon the sun appeared so out came the pneumatic drill
And it was good-bye to the smooth road surface when it came to the infill.
But, eventually, the new tarmac became embedded in the old
Leaving a scar upon the roadway for all and sundry to behold.

The Electricity Board came next to lay their cable underground
So the road was scarred again, not for the last time, we soon found
For in not too quick succession came Telecom and Water Board
And by the end that perfect road was well and truly scored.

Complaints rolled in aplenty from the residents round about
And by forming an Association they developed a certain clout.
A petition to the council ensured it came up at their meeting
And when so many residents appeared they had to call for extra seating.

After frank debate and lengthy speeches from Labour, Lib and Tory
They agreed to restore the road to former glory.
The work would start immediately and there'd be no delay
And apologies to the Association were the order of the day.

Yesterday the Council finished its resurfacing of our road.
The good news bought satisfaction and the champagne overflowed.
Then the bad news hit us hard and came without any warning
For relaying of sewers, with an EU grant, would commence in the morning!

The National Lottery

November nineteen ninety-four,
The first draw in the lottery,
Saw pools and charities galore
Take second best. It's got to be
The gamble of the century.
With sales rising to fever pitch
As selfish motives guide true sense
In bids to make the poor man rich.
We're told that charities will gain,
The arts, millennium fund and sport.
But of those who seek a win
Their efforts may just come to nought.
The fourteen million odds to one
Do not deter the fortune hunter
For who resists the game of chance
When one can be a hopeful punter?
With eyes glued to the TV screen
Each Saturday at close to eight
All semblance of a normal life
Is submerged in the random fate
Of half-a-dozen numbered balls!
So be an optimist for your weekly stake,
Mark your six numbers firm and clear
To win your share of the 'Camelot cake'.
But be warned, buy just one ticket for every draw!
Don't give way to the gambler's addiction.
Unless you use only spare cash for your bet
The lottery will cause family friction!

In Every Human Being There Is a Poet Struggling To Emerge...

The human animal has an active mind
and it's healthy to allow it to roam

But of all the pursuits it becomes involved in,
the most rewarding is writing a poem.

The voice is for speaking or singing a song,
be it 'pop' or 'O Tannenbaum'

But the brain can direct anyone's hand
to be dextrous in writing a poem.

So whether at home, in the city or town,
abroad or just crossing the 'foam'

Always find a few moments to be by yourself,
to relax and compose a poem.

If you travel to Italy you may conform
to the old and wise saw 'When in Rome'

Yet there's nothing to stop you being yourself,
sitting down and composing a poem.

You may visit the capital of our fair land
and be awestruck by St Paul's great dome.

If the 'whispering gallery' enthuses you
write your thoughts in the form of a poem.

An habitual reader you may well be,
so the next time you complete a tome

Use it as the base for intelligent thought
and convert it into a poem.

The diminutive spirits of subterranean race;
salamander, sylph, nymph and gnome,

Guard the most precious treasures of our earth
so honour their work in a poem.

In spite of your travels to work or abroad
you'll spend most of your leisure at home.

There's no finer training of a person's mind
than to sit down and write a poem.

A Whistle Stop Tour of the 1930s

One room only heated,
Ice-cold sheets on the bed.
Donkey stone for the front step.
For the grate, just blacklead.
Paid work hard to come by,
Bored with nothing to do.
Houses built semi-detached
With an external loo.
Hardship taken for granted
No such thing as 'stress',
Families made own entertainment
News from wet-battery wireless.
The cinema on Saturday mornings,
Cliffhangers for children's viewing.
Very popular they were,
Remember the youngsters queuing?
Comic films a further attraction
Though, by modern standards, slow.
The Three Stooges took centre stage.
Remember Curly, Larry and Mo?
Day excursions to the seaside,
On a train powered by steam,

To enjoy the sea, sand and sunshine,
Punch and Judy shows were a dream.
Pocket money was non-existent,
A penny earned was not strange.
Should you possess a whole tanner
It bought sweets, cigs, pop, and some change.
We were poor yet happy
And should children cause folks bother
Local Bobbies 'clipped their ears'
Parents gave them another.
Pavements served only pedestrians
And not cyclists as well.
If you rode a cycle
Then you had to have a bell.
We played outside in all weathers
At hopscotch and whipping-top.
Cards were collected from cigarette packs
By buying, winning or swop.
We played blocko, kiss catching and 'egg if you move'
When three eggs took you through the mill.
There everyone delivered blows to your rump.
Oh the bruises! I remember them still.

SOL... Save Our Libraries

The greatest gift to humans of a perceptible kind,
If you ignore a healthy body must be an educated mind.
To achieve it one must access gain to the written word
And the provision of free libraries ensure that gift is shared.

So, please don't close our libraries, even for three weeks in the year,
For access to the written text is what the literate hold dear.
Regular weekly visits to this common seat of learning
Becomes so habit-forming and avid readers are 'not for turning'.

From childhood to senior citizen there can be no better way
To self-educate and learn, without huge sums to pay.
Good readers become very good and it is often said
That even those without blue blood can be royally well-read.

For fictionalised narrative or a course of studious deployment
A library's comprehensive offering provides the stimulus for enjoyment.
From the newspapers, changed daily, video tapes and talking books
To the large print for the weak-eyed, a library's more than what it looks.

You can use a library's services to fax or photocopy there
Or visit the reference section to research books which are quite rare.
It's a haven of peace and quiet from the hubbub of the street
And a place of warmth and welcome where like-minded 'bookworms' meet.

The message to the County Council is "Don't close the library doors
E'en for three weeks of the year!" To residents "Claim what rightfully is yours,
The right to visit the library whenever you should choose."
For if the service you don't use, the library you may lose!

If active leisure pursuits allow one's body to unwind
Passive library-book reading provides exercise for the mind.
Whether nine or ninety, regardless of one's library choice,
Public Libraries can supply it. Silent readers raise one voice!

A Convulse of Comedians

I would love to have earned my living on stage.
A comedian I wanted to be.
But I treasure the pleasure I have enjoyed
From both radio and TV.

The comedian's art is not easily defined,
Over laughter and smiles he presides,
But beneath the happy-go-lucky air
There is often a sadness one hides.

So I settled for what was the best of both worlds
And enjoyed the humour of others
Brought to my home by broadcasting airwaves
So avoiding the traumatic bothers.

There's much pathos in situations comic
As we analyse the comedy scene
And, at exploiting this aspect of their art,
Both Chaplin and Wisdom were supreme.

Double acts have been numerous throughout the years
One acting as straight stooge to feed
The second comedian with the joke script
And to allow the whole act to proceed.

Where would Bud Flanagan have been without Allen?
Without Little would Large demise?
As Askey relied on 'Stinker' Murdoch
For Eric Morecambe to have 'Ernie' was wise!

Laurel and Hardy of silver screen fame,
Were both comedians within their film home
Each feeding from the other to create humour
Based on a 'villain and victim' syndrome.

This also applied to Jack Warner's sisters.
Elsie and Doris had what it takes
And what a delight, with their repartee,
Were Eric Sykes and Hattie Jacques,

But stand-up comedians operating alone
To succeed have to be simply super
And for me the one who ranks as the best
Is the late lamented Tommy Cooper.

His magical tricks, though failing to work,
Were hilarious and so was his chat.
Standing over six feet with his fez on his head
He performed with deadpan 'just like that!'

Harry Worth was a 'caution' who couldn't resist
With corner windows to play around.
By raising one arm and one foot in the air
He appeared with both feet off the ground.

Frank Randall was saucy with his old man's act
And a spittoon was a must without doubt.
Rob Wilton was guilty of procrastination
As he told of 'the day war broke out!'

ITMA was the vehicle of Tommy Handley
Which he used for his quick-fired wit
And it was due, entirely, to radio shows
Which gave Kens -Williams and Horne- such a hit.

Sandy Powell continued into old age
With his catch phrase 'Can you hear me, mother?'
Ken Platt was 'proper poorly' in his stage act
And Jack Warner had 'Sid' for a brother.

Bob Hope's line in chat was most topical
And spent much of his time 'on the road...!'
Jack Benny was miserly to the extreme
And appealed to us all by his mode.

Frankie Howerd was master of innuendo.
Benny Hill was known for saucy sketches.
Max Miller was banned for the odd indiscretion.
Mayall and Edmondson portrayed two lechers.

Sid Field based his acts on his dislike of kids
And he spoke all his lines with a drawl.
Another who used his voice to good effect
Was the diminutive, but clever, Max Wall.

Arthur English, the spiv of the World War years.
Had a humour to suit any stage.
He spoke 'gibberish' at a very fast pace
Prior to leaving with "Open the cage!"

Prof Stanley Unwin spoke Unwinese
And astounded his guests with the pace.
Little Fred Davis spoke with a lisp
With his humour based on 'Parrot face'.

Milligan, Secombe and Sellers were stars.
Individually their talents would glow
But put them together in front of a mike
And, hey-presto, you had the 'Goon Show'.

The Marx Brothers were five with incredible names.
The best known, undoubtedly, Groucho.
The Three Stooges relied on 'dumb violence'
Be it Curly or Larry or Mo!

The dear Western Brothers, with their topical verse,
Had southern accents and were upper-class lads.
They told tales of the gentry, at their expense,
And referred to the audience as 'cads'.

Rowan Atkinson's humour is achieved mainly through mime
With his characterisation, the inept Mr Bean.
Dudley Moore, Peter Cooke, Les Dawson, Victoria Wood
Have all left their mark on the comedy scene.

Ken Dodd was a student of humour and wit,
Lenny Henry fronted 'Comic Relief'
Charlie Williams' racist jokes made fun of himself,
Monty Python's gang 'beggar belief'

From Keaton to Goodwin and Lipman to French,
Joanna Lumley, Jennifer Saunders and all,
It was Flanders and Swann who provided relief'
'When the gasman came to call!'

Ted Ray was confident as Will Hay was unsure,
Jimmy Edwards euphonic, Bernard Manning so blue.
Frank Carson was raucous, Leslie Phillips demure
And sprightly Cad Robinson was better known as Cardew.

Warren Mitchell, in truth, became Alf Garnett
The xenophobe whose humour was crude.
He relied on the torpid Dandy Nichols,
'The silly moo' to whom he was rude.

Monkhouse was an utter perfectionist,
Show business had been his whole life.
As both stand-up comedian and game show host
His wit was as sharp as a knife.

Tony Hancock was the lad who lived in East Cheam
Well remembered for his part in 'The Blood Donor'.
With Sid James he plied his skills in numerous sketches.
However, like many comics, in life he was a loner.

For those I have missed I apologise
For my memory is now wearing thin
But to cure the inevitable cares of the world
I think laughter is the best medicine.

www.ingramcontent.com/pod-product-compliance
Lightning Source LLC
Chambersburg PA
CBHW051830040426
42447CB00006B/457